Psychiatric Aspects of Justification, Excuse and Mitigation in Anglo-American Criminal Law

Forensic Focus

This series, edited by Gwen Adshead, takes the field of Forensic Psychotherapy as its focal point, offering a forum for the presentation of theoretical and clinical issues. It also embraces such influential neighbouring disciplines as language, law, literature, criminology, ethics and philosophy, as well as psychiatry and psychology, its established progenitors.

Forensic Focus 17

Psychiatric Aspects of Justification, Excuse and Mitigation in Anglo-American Criminal Law

Alec Buchanan

Jessica Kingsley Publishers
London and Philadelphia

This edition published in the United Kingdom in 2000 by
Jessica Kingsley Publishers Ltd,
116 Pentonville Road,
London N1 9JB, England
and
325 Chestnut Street,
Philadelphia, PA 19106, USA.

www.jkp.com

Copyright © 2000 Alec Buchanan

Library of Congress Cataloging-in-Publication Data
Buchanan, Alec.
 Psychiatric aspects of justification, excuse, and mitigation : the jurisprudence of mental abnormality in Anglo-American criminal law / Alec Buchanan.
   p. cm. -- (Forensic focus ; 17)
  Includes bibliographical references and index.
  ISBN 1-85302-797-9 (pb : alk. paper)
   1. Insanity--Jurisprudence--United States. 2. Insanity--Jurisprudence--Great Britain. I. Title. II. Series.
 KF9242.B83 1999
 345.73'04--dc21   99-042862

British Library Cataloguing in Publication Data
Buchanan, Alec.
 Psychiatric aspects of justification, excuse, and mitigation : the jurisprudence of mental abnormality in Anglo-American criminal law. - (Forensic focus ; 17)
 1. Insanity - Jurisprudence - England 2. Insanity - Jurisprudence - United States 4. Forensic psychiatry 5. Justification (Law) 6. Extenuating circumstances
 I. Title
 345'.04
 ISBN 1853027979

ISBN 1 85302 797 9

Printed and Bound in Great Britain by
Athenaeum Press, Gateshead, Tyne and Wear

Contents

To Teresa Anne

Preface and Acknowledgements

I argue here for certain principles against which the adequacy of the criminal law's treatment of mentally abnormal offenders should be judged and for some alternatives to current provision. The argument draws on material from a range of sources including philosophy, criminology, the law and psychology as well as psychiatry. I have not attempted to provide a comprehensive description of the law; this has already been done, most notably in England by Professor Ronnie MacKay. Nor have I sought to provide detailed reviews of the other specialist areas upon which I have touched. I hope that, as a result, the trail of the argument remains visible.

The book is a development of work which I undertook at the Institute of Criminology in Cambridge while in receipt of a training fellowship funded by the Special Hospitals Service Authority. I am indebted to the librarian, Helen Krarup, and the Institute staff. Professor John Spencer, Mr Graham Virgo and Professor Tony Smith read and commented upon earlier versions of the manuscript. My thanks are due also to Professor John Gunn of the Department of Forensic Psychiatry at the Institute of Psychiatry and Dr Paul Bowden of the Maudsley Hospital. Dr Gwen Adshead encouraged my interest in this area soon after I started to train as a psychiatrist.

Professor Nigel Walker supervised my work in Cambridge, was a constant source of support and constructive criticism and encouraged me to think. Mine is the responsibility, criminal or otherwise, for errors and infelicities caused by my failing to do so.

CHAPTER 1

Preliminaries

A SUITABLE CASE FOR PUNISHMENT

Higgs, the central character of Samuel Butler's *Erewhon*, finds himself in a country where criminality is regarded as a sign of ill-health, and illness as deserving of moral opprobrium. He attends the trial of a man charged with pulmonary consumption. The man's incessant coughing counts against him, as does his previous conviction for aggravated bronchitis; he is convicted and sentenced to a lifetime of hard labour (Butler 1872, pp.95–101). At the end of the book Higgs, facing prosecution for catching measles, is forced to flee.

Erewhon is an allegory in which our usual practices of punishing and caring are reversed. It requires the reader to address the question of how we allocate punishment. Evidently, the criteria which we use are different from those employed in *Erewhon*. Falling ill does not constitute a crime. Similarly, the sympathy which we offer to the sick is dependent not on their having done something wrong, but on their being the victims of circumstance. We withdraw some of our benevolence when we discover that someone caused their own illness or sustained their injury while attacking someone else.

How, then, do we allocate punishment? We seem to do so in three stages. First, we identify a type of behaviour as a prohibited act. Second, if the punishment is to be severe, we require the perpetrator of such an act to have meant to engage in it. We do not usually punish severely those who did what they did by accident. We make exceptions to this, however. Showing that what one did was accidental will not always suffice to avoid punishment. When a man is equipped with a car or a gun, for instance, we expect him to take particular care. If he does not, and he hits someone with his car or shoots them with his gun, we may wish to punish him for his carelessness, although he meant no harm. Third, even when a prohibited act has taken place and we have identified a culprit who meant to do that act, we withhold or reduce punishment in some circumstances. We regard as less culpable, for instance, those who acted violently when they were defending themselves, provoked or insane.

We distinguish those who are punishable from those who are not, therefore, using three criteria. The first two are positive: those who are punishable have committed a prohibited act and, in the case of serious crimes, meant it. The third is negative: those who are punishable have failed to fulfil any of the criteria which would exempt them. Butler could satirise a society which failed properly to make such a distinction because we find such a failure unsatisfactory, even absurd.

LEGAL MECHANISMS

These three requirements – of a prohibited act, an actor who meant to do it and a group of exemptions for special cases – are reflected in Anglo-American criminal law. For each offence, statute or common law describes the prohibited act. The law deals with the second requirement, that the actor should have meant to do what he did, by introducing a mental element into the definition of serious offences.[1] Thus the prosecution may be required to prove that the defendant intended the act. The caveat above, that acting without intent does not necessarily stop people blaming you for what you have done, is also reflected in the law. Some offences have as their mental elements recklessness or negligence. One does not need to have intended to kill or even harm someone in order to be convicted of manslaughter after killing a pedestrian with one's car.

The third requirement is that certain exceptions be made to the general rule that someone who commits a prohibited act and fulfils the conditions of the mental element is culpable. This is dealt with in two ways. First, the 'general defences', of which self-defence and insanity are examples, are available whatever charge the defendant is facing.[2] Second, some defences are specific to particular offences. In England and Wales, someone who kills when provoked is guilty not of murder, but of manslaughter. Similar provision is made for those whose responsibility is felt by the jury to be reduced by virtue of mental abnormality through the partial defence of diminished responsibility (see p.54). This book will examine the ways in which psychiatric factors affect the degree to which it is appropriate to punish.

But what is to count as a 'psychiatric factor'? Psychiatry is a profession, a branch of medicine and an area of study. The object of that study has been variously described as mental abnormality, mental disorder, mental illness and mental disease. These terms are used widely in everyday speech, where their meanings overlap. They also have legal significance. The Mental Health Act 1983 in England and Wales uses the term 'mental disorder' to cover mental illness, psychopathic disorder, mental subnormality and 'any other disability of mind'. And individual authors generate their own definitions. The term 'mental illness', according to Moore (1984, p.245), implies irrationality. 'Mental disorder', on the other hand, is a term used by doctors to refer to conditions which they treat. For this reason, Moore argues, mental illness is a fit basis on which to excuse, whereas mental disorder is not. In this book the terms 'mental disorder', 'mental abnormality' and 'psychiatric disorder' will be used interchangeably to refer to any aspect of the mental state of an actor which is abnormal.

How can the courts, when sentencing, make allowance for a defendant's abnormal mental state? Hart identified three ways in which someone who commits an offence may be treated more leniently than would otherwise be the case (1968, p.13). First, he can argue that his actions were justified. Second, he can argue that although his actions were unjustified, he deserves to be excused. Finally, in the absence of a justification or excuse which will lead to his avoiding conviction, a defendant's sentence may still be 'mitigated'; that is, reduced in severity. The influence of psychiatric factors in these three areas will be examined.

WHAT IS DETERMINISM AND WHY DOES IT MATTER?

One of the ways that psychiatric factors influence the way in which a defendant is treated by the courts is by calling into question the degree to which he can be held responsible for what he has done. The law assumes that a defendant did what he did of his own free will. Psychiatric factors may render this assumption unsafe and thereby offer the defendant an excuse. Some have argued, however, that free will is an illusion.[3] In the eighteenth century, the Necessarians held that 'there is some fixed law of nature respecting the will, as well as the other powers of the mind, and every thing else in the constitution of nature; ...so that every volition, or choice, is constantly regulated, and determined, by what precedes it' (Priestley 1777, pp.7–8). This philosophical position is known as determinism.

In the eyes of Kupperman (1978, p.166), to say that we are determined is to say that, given the antecedent conditions of our actions, we can act in no other way than that in which we do. Hart notes that determinists hold human conduct, including the psychological components of that conduct such as decisions and choices, to be subject to certain types of law, where law is to be understood in the scientific sense (1968, p.29). One qualification has to be applied to Hart's laws if we are to be able to act in no other way from that in which we do. Some laws are probabilistic; that is, they say only that, given a series of antecedent conditions, there is a certain chance that something will happen. From the point of view of determinism, the laws which govern human conduct must be more certain than this. They must say that, given A and B are present, C has to follow.[4]

An acceptance of the truth of determinism does not inevitably lead to the abandonment of the first criterion for punishment described above; namely, the commission of a prohibited act. The Necessarians, for instance, thought that punishment should still be dispensed to the perpetrators of such acts for the good of society. Their beliefs led them to the conclusion that those punished would not have had any choice but to act as they did. It might seem unfair to punish in these circumstances[5] but, to a Necessarian, seeming unfairness was something which would just have to be tolerated. An acceptance of the truth of determinism does, however, call into question the validity of the second and third criteria for punishment. As described above, the second requires that the mental element of the offence be present, and the third provides exemptions to certain classes of defendant.

One task of these criteria is to identify those who have carried out a prohibited act but who, by virtue of the circumstances in which the act took place, were justified. The next chapter will discuss the ways in which the general defences of self-defence and necessity function as justifications. The other task of the second and third criteria for punishment is to establish whether someone can be held responsible for what he has done, or whether, by virtue of his having acted under one of the excusing conditions, he cannot.[6] The excusing conditions include being unconscious, being mistaken as to the circumstances or the consequences of one's actions, coercion and some forms of mental illness. As will also be discussed in the next chapter, they excuse probably because, when they are present, the actor's ability to choose is impaired or absent.

If all our actions are governed by laws applied to antecedent conditions, however, no distinction exists in terms of responsibility between those whose choice was normal and those whose choice was impaired. Terms such as 'he meant to do it' and 'he intended to do it' have no meaning except as descriptions of incidental mental phenomena. They contribute nothing to the explanation of *why* something happened. Nor, a determinist could argue, do the laws by which we are determined have to be known. Unless we have grounds for thinking that there are no such laws, or that such laws are never more than probabilistic, we have no reason to allow justice to hinge on the presence or absence of excuses (see Hart 1968, pp.30–31).

Students of human behaviour spend much of their time looking for just the type of laws which Hart describes. In their clinical practice, psychiatrists and psychologists think along largely determinist lines. The use of psychiatric diagnoses to predict outcome, for instance, implies that future mental states can be predicted, and, at least in part, explained in terms of antecedent conditions and scientific laws. Freud, for one, did not doubt that the issues raised by determinism needed to be confronted, or, indeed, which side of the fence he would be on when this happened: 'Once before I ventured to tell you that you nourish a deeply rooted faith in undetermined psychical events and in free will, but that this is quite unscientific and must yield to the demand of determinism whose rule extends over mental life' (Freud 1916, p.106). Psychiatrists have been equally keen to view human behaviour as governed by laws. In the words of one, 'no theory of mental medicine could develop without the working hypothesis of determinism' (Slater 1954, p.717). The conduct of an individual is governed by his mental and physical states, and these are in turn the products of antecedent mental and physical states.

This gulf, between the determinism of psychiatry and the requirement of the criminal law that humans be seen as acting freely, was remarked upon, with a hint as to where his own allegiance lay, by Judge Levin in the United States:

> Psychiatry and law approach the problem of human behavior from different philosophical perspectives. Psychiatry purports to be scientific and takes a deterministic position with regard to behavior. Its view of human nature is expressed in terms of drives and dispositions which, like mechanical forces, operate in accordance with universal laws of causation...criminal law is, however, a practical, rational, normative science which, although it draws upon theoretical science, also is concerned to pass judgement on human conduct. Its view of human nature asserts the reality of free choice and rejects the thesis that the conduct of normal adults is a mere expression of imperious psychological necessity. Given the additional purpose to evaluate conduct, some degree of autonomy is a necessary postulate. (*Pollard* v. *United States* at 479–480)[7]

A legal system which accepted the tenets of determinism would be very different from that which presently comprises Anglo-American criminal law. The current meaning of guilt – that the defendant can properly be held responsible for what he has done – would be lost. Trials would establish merely whether the accused did the deed in question. The verdict would be not one of 'guilty' or 'not guilty', but of 'did it' or 'did not do it'. Issues such as whether or not the person had a gun at his back or was in a mental state which precluded his ability to choose could be dealt with at a later, sentencing, stage.[8] It is doubtful whether the sentence would be described as punishment (except, perhaps, by the defendant) since it seems inhumane to punish those who could not have avoided doing what they did.[9] Detention would be justified instead in terms of public protection or deterrence. Our present concepts of guilt, justification and excuse would disappear and much of the jury's traditional role in the trial would be removed.

THE ARGUMENTS AGAINST DETERMINISM

Several arguments have been put forward to refute the determinist position and to support the legal recognition of excusing conditions. Some, such as those advanced by Dennett (1973) and Planck (1933), are 'compatibilist'. Dennett and Planck do not deny that some aspects of human behaviour can be explained in determinist terms by applying laws to antecedent conditions. They maintain, however, that 'free will' explanations, couched in terms of choice and purpose, are also of value. Other authors, such as Kupperman and Hart, do not think that free will is compatible with determinism and feel obliged to make a choice between the two approaches.

Dennett's (1973) view is that deterministic explanations, on the one hand, and explanations of behaviour in terms of purpose, on the other, are not mutually exclusive. The example which he gives is that of a chess-playing computer. In attempting to predict the computer's next move we can adopt several 'stances'. One, the physical stance, involves dismantling the computer and studying its components in sufficient detail to allow the prediction of its response in every situation. Another is the intentional stance, which involves making an assumption that the computer has been programmed to play rationally. Using this assumption one can then proceed to predict what it will do.[10]

The physical stance is analogous to determinism. Predictions are made by applying scientific laws to conditions in different parts of the computer. The occurrence of a certain voltage in one component will result in a certain current passing in another. There is no need to take into account what the designer intended. The intentional stance, on the other hand, is analogous to a belief in free will. It assumes that the designer made choices as to how the computer would behave. This assumption allows us to predict the machine's next move without knowing the details of its construction. Both the physical stance and the intentional stance are valid, Dennett argues, and there is no reason to think that one can displace the other.

It is unlikely, however, that Dennett's two approaches will be equally successful in all circumstances. The intentional stance would be adequate when one move was clearly better than all of the others, but might fail to predict the computer's behaviour if the situation on the board was complicated and each of several moves seemed to offer its own advantages. It seems to me also that the threat to our present practices of blaming and excusing comes not from the suggestion that human behaviour can be predicted using determinist principles, but from the suggestion that such principles can be used to explain why certain types of behaviour occur. Explanation is not simply prediction. Some things, such as the acquisition of language by children, we can predict without being able to explain.

Dennett himself offers the example of a man who stops saying the word 'father'. The layman's 'intentional-stance' explanation, that he is doing so as a part of a bet, has the rug pulled from under it when the man is found to have suffered a haemorrhage in that part of his cerebral cortex which controls speech. It is clear that in such instances 'physical-stance' and 'intentional-stance' explanations do not simply coexist. While the two may be compatible when the task is one of prediction, they are less so when an explanation is required. Determinists argue that, as medical science advances, the role of the intentional stance in the explanation of human behaviour will contract, and that of the physical stance will expand. Dennett's arguments do not seem to deny this possibility.[11]

In the view of Planck, to ask whether the human will is free or determined is to be guilty of an 'inadmissible logical disjunction' (1933, p.102). On the one hand, in our dealings with others we proceed on the basis that their words and actions are determined by distinct and identifiable causes. Some of these we can manipulate: we know how to provoke anger and how to induce fear. We assume that if we were more insightful we could see how someone's genes and upbringing had caused long-lasting traits, such as nervousness, to appear. On the other hand, when we say that our will is free we refer to the fact that we have the opportunity to choose when making decisions. These two observations, one concerning our attitude to others and the other concerning our awareness of self, are not mutually exclusive. They would only be so, Planck argues, if we could see ourselves perfectly. Such successful introspection is logically excluded, however, since the object and the subject of an act of knowing can never be identical.[12] To ask if the law of causality can be applied to one's own will is to ask if someone could lift himself above himself or outrun his own shadow. His conclusion on the subject is brief: 'In summary, we can therefore say: observed from without, the will is causally determined. Observed from within, it is free. This finding takes care of the problem of the freedom of the will' (1950, p.75).

Planck's finding takes care of the problem in the sense that it explains how we manage simultaneously to think in terms of determinism and free will. It does not, however, take care of the problem of deciding which of these philosophical positions should be reflected in our legal system. If, as he suggests, the only reason we feel free is our inadequate self-perception, why should we assume for the purposes of the criminal law that defendants have free will? It seems equally reasonable to assume that their actions are causally determined, particularly since in most cases someone else will be on trial and not us. We will be observing 'from without'.

These 'compatibilist' arguments, therefore, fail to explain why we have a system of criminal law which assumes we are free to choose. Our preference for such a system is easily explained, however, if the determinist position – that human behaviour can be explained by applying laws to antecedent conditions – is incorrect. Kupperman (1978, pp.171, 174–175) argues that the mental states associated with acting – mood states, decisions, choices and so on – defy precise description. Since these mental states form the antecedent conditions upon which any proposed laws of human behaviour must operate, it becomes impossible, due to the inadequacy of any description of these states, to derive such laws.

The example he uses is that of a man who is considering leaving his job. It might be possible, Kupperman concedes, to derive a law whereby in conditions which include the offer of a better-paying job elsewhere, if a man is in a mood that could be termed 'anger with his boss', he will quit. But what if his attitude to his boss is one not of anger but of 'amused but affectionate irritation'? Even if we can predict that given certain conditions a man will engage in a particular course of action, we cannot predict his behaviour in all circumstances. This problem will not go away for as long as 'amused but affectionate irritation' and other mood states which affect our behaviour remain difficult to measure.

Kupperman makes a convincing case that it is not possible, given the present state of knowledge, to derive most of human behaviour by applying scientific laws to a set of pre-existing conditions. He does not, however, make a case for assuming at law that our behaviour is the result of free will. Indeed, he concedes that in the future 'it may be possible...to arrive at some causal laws of the sort desired' (1978, p.175). In Kupperman's view, the question of whether or not our actions are determined is essentially an empirical one. For the present we should assume that we have free will. The scientists, however, may yet prove to us that in some instances this is an illusion. 'The issue is one of facts,' writes Kupperman. His conclusion, that we should assume that our wills are free, is arrived at 'on the basis of present evidence' (p.178).

Hart (1968, pp.28–53), like Kupperman, regards as moot the question of whether determinism is true. His solution, however, avoids the fragility of Kupperman's 'empiricist' position. Hart notes the similarity between conditions which the criminal law regards as 'excusing' – accident, mistake, provocation, duress and insanity – and those which are regarded as 'invalidating' such civil transactions as wills, marriages, gifts and contracts. He then asks why it is that we value a criminal justice system which takes excusing conditions into account.

The first possibility which Hart identifies is that the requirement for excuses is derivative, stemming from a more fundamental requirement that, in order for criminal responsibility to exist, there must be moral responsibility. We wish to ensure, before a prosecution can be successful, not only that someone intended to act in the way he did, but that he intended to do wrong. We take into account excuses because they cast doubt on this intentional wrongness. This view, that the law exists to punish not only acts which are simply forbidden, but acts which are morally wrong, has been expressed by jurisprudential authorities on both sides of the Atlantic.[13] Hart argues that it is incorrect, and points out that the law defines as offences numerous forms of behaviour whose moral wrongness is, at best, in doubt.[14]

The second possible reason, which Hart examines, for our desire to convict only the 'mentally responsible' relates to what he calls Bentham's 'economy of threats'. Bentham thought that it was wrong to punish where the threat of punishment could not have deterred a potential offender from indulging in criminal behaviour in general, or in the particular act for which he was being tried (Bentham 1823, pp.1–13). Punishment in such cases was wasteful because suffering was caused to the accused in circumstances where it could do no good. Hart's argument in reply is that it is in fact far from clear that making punishment dependent on responsibility is the most efficient way of persuading the members of a society to observe the law. Doing away with 'accident' as an excuse, for instance, might make everybody take more care.[15] We recognise excuses despite the possibility that they in this way decrease the effectiveness of the law. Hart concludes that we do not see the legal system simply as a means of guiding the individual into conformity.

Instead, he argues, the criminal law is best seen as a choosing system in which individuals are aware of the costs and benefits of various courses of action. At this point he returns to the similarities, described earlier, between conditions which excuse under the criminal law and those which invalidate marriages, contracts and wills. In the absence of such invalidating conditions as accident, mistake and insanity, contracts entered into without the individual making a real choice would remain in force and the individual would suffer a corresponding loss of control over his or her future. Similarly, by attaching excusing conditions to criminal responsibility, we maximise the chances of an individual successfully predicting whether sanctions will be applied to him and choice, at least perceived choice, becomes one of the factors which determines whether such sanctions will be applied. To Hart, no form of determinism can throw doubt on the satisfaction which individuals derive from such a system.

This seems the most convincing explanation why there has developed in Anglo-American law a system which excludes from punishment, or reduces the punishment dispensed to, those who act under excusing conditions. It is also a good argument for the continuance of such a system. Hart would have to concede, however, that although determinists cannot deny the satisfaction gained from seeing one's choices rendered effective, they can argue that in some instances such satisfaction is misplaced. To return to the example described earlier, that of the man who stopped saying the word 'father', a third party, and perhaps the man himself, might assume that he stopped out of choice, only for it to be shown subsequently that the probable cause of his stopping was a cerebral haemorrhage. It seems impossible to deny that in such a case a mechanical, deterministic explanation has replaced a purposive, intentional one.

There is reason to doubt, however, that in the future such deterministic inroads into what Dennett (1973, p.182) calls the 'domain' of intentional explanation will be substantial, or even the norm. As one Royal Commission (1957, p.127) pointed out, the task of applying medical evidence to legal concepts has been relatively immune to scientific advances. Kupperman (1978, p.166) notes, without making much of it, that the trend in medical thinking on drug addiction has been away from the notion that addicts are not free with respect to their drug habit towards the idea that addiction can be overcome by will-power. We are likely to continue to require, as a condition of punishment, responsibility for a criminal act. A criminal justice system which reflects this requirement must take into account, when assessing culpability, the defendant's mental state at the time he acted.

STRUCTURE OF THE BOOK

This book addresses the question of how psychiatric disorders influence the processes of justification, excuse and mitigation in Anglo-American criminal law. There are other approaches to examining the differences in the way in which mentally disordered defendants are treated by the courts. Some reviewers structure their discussion around each of the defences in turn. One aim of this book, however, is to discuss the degree to which present provision for the mentally disordered adequately reflects the principles which govern the distribution of punishment. Hart identified these as justification, excuse and mitigation (Hart 1968, p.13; see also p.13 above).

The first thing to be established is what we mean by justification, excuse and mitigation. This will be addressed in Chapters 2 and 3; Chapter 3 will also examine the ways in which psychiatric factors can contribute to mitigation. The means by which psychiatric factors provide excuses will be discussed in Chapter 4. The ways in which Anglo-American law takes into account these excuses will be covered in Chapter 5. Chapter 6 will discuss the principles at work, and Chapter 7 some alternatives to the present arrangements.

NOTES

1. For less serious offences, however, this 'mental element' is not required, and a defendant may be convicted in the absence of intention, knowledge, recklessness or negligence. Examples include purveying unsound meat, dispensing medicines on an invalid prescription and selling intoxicating liquor to someone who is drunk. These offences are said to carry 'strict liability'. Legal authorities point out that liability in such cases, although 'strict', is not 'absolute' (see Smith and Hogan 1996, pp.101–102). This is because the general defences, such as automatism and insanity, are still available. In addition, defendants avoid conviction for some offences where there is evidence that they demonstrated due diligence (see Ashworth 1995a, pp.158–167; for reviews see Richardson 1999, ss.17.1–17.9; Smith and Hogan 1996, pp.101–125).

2. Robinson (1982) has analysed the range of defences available.

3. The lawyers for an American man, sentenced to death and appealing to the Supreme Court, argued that his killing the manager of a pizza store was the result not of free will but of a genetic predisposition to violence (*The Independent on Sunday*, 12 February 1995, p.19).

4. Scruton (1994, p.228) thinks any determinist who holds that events are determined in a probabilistic sense only concedes the argument to the advocates of free will.

5. Priestley's (1777, pp.73–96) view was criticised by his contemporary, John Palmer (1779).

6. The term 'excusing condition' is Hart's (1968, p.28). Some legal theorists question whether all of these excusing conditions are, in the legal sense, excuses (see p.22 below).

7. Judge Levin was quoting extensively from Hall (1956).

8. In other words, these issues would be dealt with in the context of mitigation. Such a system has been suggested by Baroness Wootton (Wootton 1959, pp.266, 267; 1963, pp.46–57; 1960). Baroness Wootton's views have in turn been criticised by Hart (1968, pp.193–209).

9. Even under present provision, however, some such defendants are found guilty. In *Elliot* v. *C.* a backward 14-year-old was held to have acted recklessly and so was convicted of arson by a court which acknowledged the possibility that her backwardness rendered her incapable of considering the relevant risk. *R.* v. *Reid* [1992], a reckless driving case, suggested that a defendant who acted under an 'understandable and excusable mistake' was not reckless (at 393). The Court

of Appeal has subsequently confirmed, however, that for recklessness to be present there is no need for the defendant to appreciate the risk (see *R. v. Coles*).

10. Dennett also offers a third option, which he labels the 'design stance'. Followers of this approach would proceed directly to the computer program in order to predict how the machine would react. This sounds like cheating.

11. Later in his essay, Dennett seems to acknowledge this. He refers to the 'partial erosion of the Intentional domain, an eventuality against which there are no conceptual guarantees at all' (1973, p.182). It is difficult to reconcile this statement with his earlier assertion that the 'physical stance' does not displace explanations couched in terms of the actor's intention or purpose in doing as he did.

12. One could quibble with this: we speak of someone 'knowing their own mind', suggesting that in some instances the subject and the object of knowing can be identical. But the substance of Planck's point stands. Even if one knows one's own mind, it is difficult to see how one could fully know the part which does the knowing.

13. In England, Lord Denning said: 'In order for an act to be punishable, it must be morally blameworthy. It must be a sin' (Denning 1953, p.112). In the United States, Hall (1947, p.103) has argued that the general principle of liability is that, for conviction, there be proved the 'voluntary doing of a morally wrong act'.

14. Hart cites as an example legislation intended to give effect to a state monopoly of road or rail transport.

15. See the arguments in favour of strict liability cited by Ashworth (1995a, pp.160–162).

CHAPTER 2

The Theory of Justification and Excuse

If I have done something which would usually be considered criminal, there are two ways in which I may avoid punishment without denying that I was to blame for what happened. The 'offence' may have occurred a long time ago and prosecution may therefore be ruled out by law or custom.[1] Or, principles of double jeopardy may apply because I have been convicted and sentenced. In general, however, I need a defence which denies that I am, in this instance at least, a fit subject for punishment. This is called an 'exculpatory' defence, and has to amount either to a justification or to an excuse (Duff 1990, p.78; Williams 1982, p.732).

Some legal theorists dispute this analysis, however, arguing that one can avoid punishment without presenting either a justification or an excuse. Robinson (1982) has distinguished justifications and excuses, on the one hand, from a failure on the part of the prosecution to prove the 'elements' of the offence, on the other. Tur (1993) holds that 'lawful excuse' is always a secondary matter, to be dealt with after the definition of the offence is satisfied (pp. 215, 216). By his argument, where intention is the mental element of a crime, those who did what they did by mistake do not need an excuse; no crime has been committed.

This assumes that Robinson's categories are mutually exclusive and that a claim that the 'elements' of an offence have not been proved cannot also be an excuse. This has been disputed (Husak 1992). Ashworth (1995a, p.240), after provisionally distinguishing denials of the fault element from excuses, concludes that they should not be regarded as belonging to separate groups. Glanville Williams (1982, p.734) has also criticised the practice of insisting on a distinction.[2] Justifications, it has similarly been argued, remain justifications even when they deny the fault element (D'Arcy 1963, p.82). The definitions of justification and excuse employed here will include instances where the fault element is denied. This approach coincides with everyday use of the term 'excuse'. When a policeman arrests the wrong man, we do not call his claim that the man looked identical to an escaped prisoner a denial of the fault element. We call it an excuse.

Although the distinction between denials of the fault element and other excuses is not one which will be pursued here, it can be of importance to a defendant. In order to deny the fault element, he is not required to produce any evidence of his own. He can avoid conviction by demonstrating only that the prosecution have not proved that element beyond reasonable doubt. Before the prosecution are required to disprove the defence of duress, however, he must satisfy the judge that there is evidence fit to be left to the jury (Richardson 1999, s.17.125).

The first part of this chapter is concerned with justification. I think that the meaning in Anglo-American law of the term 'justification' is unclear. Jurisprudential theorists on both sides of the Atlantic have addressed the issue and their conclusions will be reviewed. The operation of those general defences which work according to the principles of justification will be examined next, and the theoretical definitions of justification compared with those which emerge from the discussion of legal practice. The role of psychiatric factors will then be addressed.

The second part of the chapter will examine what it means to excuse. Although the meaning of the term itself is less in debate than is the case for justification, substantial disagreements have arisen over whom we should excuse and why we do so. The various theories which have been put forward will be discussed. The role of psychiatric factors will then be examined with reference to these theories.

JUSTIFICATION

Current confusion

Textbook definitions of justification are often unhelpful. Greenawalt (1987, p.289) contends that the defining characteristic is whether or not what the actor did was 'warranted', but does not explain what he means by this. Gordon (1978, p.423), while noting that the term is often used synonymously with excuse, states that, used correctly, justification refers to factors which deprive an act of its criminal nature: it renders lawful what would otherwise be unlawful. Excuses, on the other hand, merely render that act unpunishable.

Gordon's assertion notwithstanding, there are several ways in which excuses deny criminality. First, when the defendant acts involuntarily there is no *actus reus*,[3] yet sleep-walking is an excuse for, not a justification of, the antisocial actions of some somnambulists and may form the basis of an insanity defence (see *R. v. Burgess*). Second, when the defendant makes a mistake as to the circumstances in which he is acting, the *mens rea* of the crime may be denied by this excuse, in which case no crime is deemed to have occurred.[4] Finally, even when excuses do not deny the presence of an *actus reus* or *mens rea*, as is the case in duress,[5] it has been argued that the criminal nature of the act is being denied by a successful defence.[6]

In practice, the distinction between justification and excuse is less important than was once the case. Eighteenth-century English common law distinguished three types of killing. Felonies, whether committed with intent or culpable negligence, could be dealt with using the full force of the law. Justified killings, such as those carried out by the public hangman or to prevent the escape of a convicted felon, were not punishable. Unintentional homicides were excused unless there was evidence of culpable negligence. Successful defences of justification and excuse both led to findings of not guilty but, in the case of excuse, the defendant's goods were forfeited. Since the abolition of forfeiture in 1828, however, the composition of a successful defence has made no difference to the defendant. Whether it is based on a justification or an excuse, unless the defendant is found insane, the result has been a simple acquittal (Smith and Hogan 1996, p.193).

Whether because of the lack of clarity of some writing on the subject, or the reduced importance of the distinction in the law of England and Wales, judges, according to Ashworth (1995a, p.132), frequently confuse justification with excuse. Smith (1989, p.126) describes the distinction as of limited value in the development of the general defences. Lord Goddard seemed to be using the terms interchangeably when he dismissed an appeal on the basis that 'while the provocation would no doubt have excused a blow…it could not have justified the infliction of such injuries as…to cause three or four fractures of the skull' (R. v. McCarthy at 109, 110). What, then, is a justification?

Common usage and legal theory

We may justify a decision, a belief, a practice and a rule as well as an action. The decision to field a free-scoring but only half-fit centre forward may be justified by his scoring the winning goal. A belief that the prime minister is untrustworthy may be justified by subsequent events. In such cases little is implied concerning our moral position. When we justify a practice or a rule, however, and especially when we justify an action, we are usually offering a moral judgement (see D'Arcy 1963, p.78).

Most writers on the subject agree that the judgement concerns the rightness of a course of action.[7] They sometimes further define rightness as a product of weighing the social value of an act against the harm it causes (Smith 1989, p.53). Some imply that this process of weighing must come out in the actor's favour (Ashworth 1995a, p.145; Uniacke 1994, p.11). Others require only that it not come out against him. By this, rather wider, definition, a justified act is merely 'not wrong' (D'Arcy 1963, p.80), 'permissible' (Ashworth 1995a, p.132), or 'tolerated' (Robinson 1982, p.229). Finally, several authors point out that most of what we do we are not required to justify. A justification is only required when an action appears wrongful (D'Arcy 1963, p.79; Uniacke 1994, p.11).

This definition, whereby an act is justified if it is the right – or, at least, not the wrong – thing to do, reflects one everyday use of the word 'justification'. We say an act is justified if the good occasioned by its being done is greater than the harm. I am justified in breaking the speed limit if in doing so I get you to hospital in time to save your life. My actions are less likely to be regarded as justified if I endangered the lives of others or if your injuries were not serious. There is another use of the term 'justification', however, which does not depend on an objective balancing of harms. This use describes the adequacy of someone's reasons for acting as they did. Following this use I was justified in driving as I did if I believed that your life was in danger. Uniacke (1994, p.15) calls this 'agent-perspectival', as opposed to 'objective', justification.[8]

In many instances the same conclusions, as to whether or not a particular act is justified, will be reached whichever definition, objective balancing or 'agent-per-spectival', is used. People are justified in doing as they do when their actions are justified actions. One's reasons for acting are adequate if the good occasioned outweighs the harm. If you are injured, my breaking the speed limit is justified both in terms of the balance of good and harm and in terms of the adequacy of my reasons for acting as I did.

The two meanings diverge, however, with reference to mistakes. Where you are feigning injury as part of an elaborate practical joke, the act of speeding cannot be justified, but I could still describe my actions as 'justified in the circumstances as I believed them to be'. At least where we feel we would have done the same thing ourselves, we use the term 'justification' to refer to someone's reasons for acting, even when those reasons are based on mistaken beliefs.

When we feel that the mistake was not a reasonable one, we are less likely to describe the actor as justified. The fact that your friends were suppressing smiles rather than showing concern as they helped you into the car should have alerted me to what was going on. The bottle of fake blood, clearly labelled, which fell out of your pocket as we drove off should have made me wonder whether your injuries were genuine.[9] It would seem, however, that for reasonable mistakes at least we are capable of describing someone as 'justified in acting as they did in the circumstances' and of maintaining, simultaneously, that the deed itself was unjustified.

How, then, should justification be defined as it applies to the criminal law? One possibility is to work backwards and argue, following Gordon (1978; see also p.23 above), that a justification denies the criminal nature of the act.[10] This seems unsatisfactory for legal purposes. Surely we would prefer that a principle (justification) lead us to the denial of criminality, not the other way around. In addition, as pointed out earlier, some excuses deny that the definition of the offence is fulfilled.

A more popular definition follows the first of the two meanings of justification described here: justification, unlike excuse, appeals to an objective 'rightness'. To describe an act as justified is hence to deny that wrong has been done. Thus incorrect information can never justify (Fletcher 1978, p.766; Williams 1982, p.740). The victim of an act which is justified – a criminal being arrested, for example – is not entitled to defend himself, as opposed to the victim of an attack which is merely excused, who is (Fletcher 1978, pp.759–762; Williams 1982, p.732). Similarly, other people are entitled to assist in acts which are justified but not in acts which are excused (Fletcher 1978, pp.759–762; Williams 1982). Williams' (1982, p.741) advocacy of the objective criterion leads him to suggest that acts can be justified by reference to evidence unknown to the actor. The next section will compare the definition provided by Fletcher and Williams with the use of the term 'justification' in Anglo-American case law.

Justification in action

Justification and the general defences

Exculpatory defences[11] depend on the principles of justification and excuse (Duff 1990, p.78; Williams 1982, p.732). Unfortunately, not everyone agrees which principle is operating in which case. Self-defence is usually classified as a justification but has also been described as an excuse (Robinson 1982; Williams 1982). Necessity, it has been argued, can fulfil both roles (Robinson 1982). Provocation has been classified as a justification (McAuley 1987), an excuse (Dressler 1988), both (Alldridge 1983; Ashworth 1976) and neither (Hart 1968, pp.13–17; Robinson 1982). This disagreement as to whether particular defences are excuses or justifications presumably reflects a lack of clarity over what excuse and justification mean. Provocation will be discussed in the next chapter. In this chapter the general defence of self-defence and the doctrine of necessity will be examined in order to establish whether the legal definition of justification is the same as that which the theorists have proposed.

Necessity

Traditionally, the courts in England and Wales have been reluctant to allow defendants to avoid conviction by claiming that their actions were necessary. Hale (1736, p.54) argued that such a claim was no defence to a charge of stealing clothing. Stephen (1883, pp.108–110) thought that the defence of necessity should succeed where a justification was present but that this was rarely the case. It has been feared that allowing such defences would, in the words of Lord Denning, 'open a way through which all kinds of disorder and lawlessness would pass' (*London Borough of Southwark* v. *Williams and another* at 179). The hungry would steal for food and an Englishman's home would be legally occupied by the needy.

Nevertheless, there are instances where defendants seem to have escaped conviction by demonstrating the necessity of their acting as they did. It was a defence to the criminal charge of procuring an abortion in England and Wales to show that such action was necessary to preserve the life of the mother long before the law made statutory provision to this effect (*R. v. Bourne*). And the Court of Appeal quashed the conviction of a Mr Willer for reckless driving where the defendant drove on the pavement to escape a group of youths who were intent on attacking him (*R. v. Willer*).[12] Willer's situation is usually referred to, not as necessity, but as 'duress of circumstances' (Richardson 1999, s.17.124; Smith and Hogan 1996, p.242).[13] There is general agreement, however, that the principle underlying the decision was that his actions were necessary (Clarkson and Keating 1998, p.354; Smith and Hogan 1996, pp.248, 249).[14] It has also been argued that the courts apply the doctrine of necessity more widely than is commonly recognised; for instance, by defining intention in such a way that those who act out of necessity can be shown to lack it (see Smith 1989, pp.68–70).

To the extent that the doctrine of necessity operates in English law, what principles underlie it? Is it a justification for otherwise illegal acts or an excuse for them? Legal texts use by way of illustration a case where the defence failed. In the nineteenth century the crew of a yacht, three men and a cabin boy, were left in an open boat after the yacht sank (*R. v. Dudley and Stephens*). After three weeks, one of the men killed the boy and the three ate his remains for four days until they were rescued. Two of the men, Dudley and Stephens, were convicted of murder. The judges who tried the case concluded that it was no defence that the actions of the adult seamen were necessary to preserve their own lives. In the absence of a self-sacrificing volunteer, it was the duty of all to die.

The reports do not make clear the judges' reasons for reaching this conclusion (Simpson 1984; Smith and Hogan 1996, pp.256–258). They seem to have decided that the success of a defence of necessity hinged on there being a justification for the sailors' actions.[15] There could be no such justification because the sanctity of human life was paramount. Courts in the United States have been similarly reluctant to admit a defence of necessity where the defendant has killed someone. A seaman was prosecuted for obeying an order to throw overboard some of the occupants of an overloaded life-raft,[16] and one authority has written, with reference to such predicaments, that 'there is no rule of human jettison' (Cardozo 1947, p.390).

The defence of necessity put forward by Dudley and Stephens probably failed, therefore, because the judges thought that the sailors' killing of the boy was more wrong than risking their own deaths.[17] Although Mr Willer's predicament was less extreme, the fact that he did not actually harm anyone makes any calculation of the balance of wrongs more problematic. The sanctity of life was not at stake. What was at issue was the high chance of harm being done to Willer and to his passengers on the one hand, and the smaller chance of harm being done to a pedestrian on the other.[18] But the harm done to the pedestrian by Willer's car could well have been more serious than that done to Willer. If the defence of necessity works according to the principle of justification alone, some calculation of the relative harms of Willer's possible courses of action would have to be made. How is a jury to balance the low risk of serious harm against the higher risk of something less serious? An economist might give harm and risk a statistical value and multiply them together for each circumstance. It seems unlikely that juries do this.[19]

It seems more likely that the defence of necessity in English criminal law operates according not to one but to two principles. In R. v. Dudley and Stephens the court was concerned with the relative value of two wrongs: the killing of the cabin boy on the one hand, and the starvation of the other men in the boat on the other. The American Law Institute's Model Penal Code (1985) is similarly concerned with this balance when it states, with regard to the defence of necessity: 'conduct which the actor believes to be necessary to avoid a harm or an evil to himself or to another is justifiable, provided that the harm of the evil sought to be avoided by such conduct is greater than that sought to be prevented by the law defining the offense charged' (Article 3.02).[20] Like the court in R. v. Dudley and Stephens, the American Law Institute is equating necessity with justification. The definition of that justification, based on an objective balancing of wrongs, is consistent with the descriptions provided by legal theorists and described earlier (see p.26).

In cases such as that of Mr Willer, however, where the defendant drove on the pavement to avoid being attacked, the concern seems to be not only to establish the balance of wrongs, but also to make allowance for the pressure under which the defendant was acting. This is the sense in which Mr Willer's situation can be described as 'duress of circumstances'. Willer could be described as 'not making a proper choice', 'not in control of the situation' or 'not himself', and these, as will be discussed in the next section, are forms of excuse. Similar logic presumably led the Supreme Court of Canada to conclude that necessity operates as an excuse (and not as a justification), relying, in their view, on a 'realistic assessment of human weakness' (Perka et al. v. R. [at 2]). This is a concept of necessity very different from that described by Stephen (1883, pp.108–110), the court in R. v. Dudley and Stephens and the American Law Institute.

Self-defence

The law in England and Wales makes a distinction between the use of force in defence of oneself or others and its use in the prevention of crime. The use of force in the prevention of crime is regulated by Section Three of the Criminal Law Act 1967. Defence of oneself or others is regulated by the common law. The law permits the use of as much force as is reasonable (Clarkson and Keating 1998, p.307; Richardson 1999, ss.19.41, 19.42; Smith and Hogan 1996, p.259). In contrast to duress, where the defence is only available to defendants whose belief that they are subject to threats is a reasonable one (see *R*. v. *Graham*, *R*. v. *Howe*), defendants pleading self-defence to a charge for which the mental element is intent or recklessness need show only that they did what they honestly believed necessary (Richardson 1999, s.19.42; Smith and Hogan 1996, pp.259–260). As a consequence, mistakes, even unreasonable mistakes, can form the basis of a defence (see *R*. v. *Gladstone Williams* [where the charge was one of assault]; *R*. v. *Beckford* [murder] and; *R*. v. *Scarlett* [manslaughter]).[21]

Williams (1982, p.739) has argued that the law exculpates those whose otherwise criminal acts are undertaken in self-defence because such acts are less wrongful than would otherwise be the case. The aggressor causes what he calls 'the mischief', for one thing, and future crimes may be deterred. The requirement that the force used should be reasonable and, where the mental element required is negligence, that the actor's belief be reasonable too, would similarly suggest that self-defence is a justification. So why have some authorities referred to some actions taken in defence of oneself or others as excused? (Smith and Hogan 1992, p.252.)

There are two possible reasons. First, as discussed earlier, Fletcher and Williams take the view that incorrect information cannot justify, it can only excuse. Someone who acts in the mistaken belief that they are defending themselves should therefore be regarded as excused rather than justified. Second, the 'self-defender' may be unable to judge the relative levels of harm: he cannot be certain what his attacker is likely to do. It is asking a lot to expect a rational judgement of the levels of harm involved from someone whose life is in danger.[22] It is asking even more to expect them meekly to succumb because the only means of defence available to them would result in them doing more damage to their attacker than is justified by the harm the attacker is about to do to them, the wrongfulness of the attack or the requirements of deterrence.[23] Where someone who is in danger does more than a reasonable person would deem necessary, they may have an excuse although their actions are unjustified.

The law of self-defence in the United States is similar. The defence can be allowed on the basis of what the defendant believed to be the case. In contrast to the position adopted by Fletcher (1978, p.766) and Williams (1982, p.740), however, incorrect information has been described as capable of offering a justification. The defendant in *People* v. *Young* was a New Yorker who came across two middle-aged men struggling with a younger man. Believing that the younger man was being assaulted, Young went forcefully to his aid. The two older men turned out to be policemen and Young was convicted of criminal assault. His appeal failed when the New York Court of Appeals decided that, since the crime charged required only that the defendant intended to strike a blow, he had no defence. The majority came to no conclusion as to whether Young's actions were justified. Two dissenting judges, however, did. They argued, 'One who kills in defense of another and proffers this defence of justification is to be judged according to the circumstances as they appeared to him' (People v. Young at 5; the case is discussed by Greenawalt 1984).

The dissenting judges, Froessel and Van Voorhis, quoted several precedents. Unfortunately for present purposes, they were trying to establish whether the defence should succeed, not whether incorrect information can justify. Thus one of the precedents which they quoted makes clear only that self-defence can be based on incorrect information, not that it is then a justification (People v. Maine at 696). Another precedent consists of themselves, again in dissent, again asserting that self-defence on such grounds is justifiable (People v. Perkins at 666). Later in the judgement, however, they state that the defence can offer 'reasonable mistake' to show that the killing was not simply justifiable, but 'justifiable or excusable' (People v. Perkins at 667). It could be argued that the descriptions of justification in People v. Young reflect inexact usage by judges who were concentrating on the admissibility of a plea of self-defence, not on the definition of justification.

There are, however, other suggestions that the law allows reasonable mistakes to contribute to a justification. New York state law in the first half of the twentieth century described as 'justifiable homicide' (see People v. Maine at 696) a killing where the defendant's mistake, in believing that he was defending himself, was reasonable. Justifiable homicide is of course a legal category. Such categories, it could be argued, are of little relevance to defining the limits of justification. The American Law Institute's Model Penal Code (1985), however, also describes the use of force in defence of the self or others as justified 'in the circumstances as the actor believes them to be'. A rider adds that where this belief is 'negligently or recklessly formed', and hence, in one sense, unreasonable, prosecution again becomes possible (see American Law Institute 1985, Article 3.04. The reference to negligent or reckless mistakes appears in the explanatory note to the Article).

Implications for the definition of justification

The general defence of necessity, it has been argued here, works according to the principles of both justification and excuse. That aspect of the defence which involves balancing harms should be seen as offering a justification. That part which acknowledges the pressure under which someone acted should be seen as a form of excuse. When harms are being balanced, the requirement is that objective criteria be used. The Model Penal Code is explicit in this regard. Self-defence similarly combines justification and excuse. Here, however, American law suggests that a justification can be based on mistaken information, at least when the mistake is reasonable.

How can these two, different, legal definitions of justification be reconciled? It is possible that one usage is simply wrong: certainly, Williams (1982, p.740) and Fletcher (1978, p.766) would argue that mistakes, however reasonable, cannot justify (see p.26). It is also possible, however, that the two definitions each reflect a form of common usage. It has been argued here that, while we regard an act as justified when the good occasioned outweighs the harm, we also use the term 'justification' to describe the adequacy of someone's reasons for doing as they did. One authority has described this as 'agent-perspectival' justification (see p.25). It is this, second, meaning which is being used when the *Model Penal Code* describes reasonable mistakes as justifying self-defence.

To the extent that reasonable mistakes are allowed to justify, therefore, the definition of justification in Anglo-American law is at variance with that provided by legal theorists. In addition, the law does not follow Williams' (1982, p.741) suggestion that information unknown to the actor should be able to justify his actions. In the nineteenth century, an armed constable was keeping watch on a wood from which timber had been stolen (*R. v. Dadson*). A man emerged from the wood with some branches over his shoulder and was ordered to stop by the constable. When he failed to do so, the officer shot him in the leg. It was assumed at the time that it was justified to shoot a convicted felon in order to prevent his escape. The thief had two previous convictions for stealing wood and was therefore, by the convention of the time, a felon. This was unknown to the officer, however, who was convicted of wounding.

The precedent set by this case, that information must have been known to the actor before it can contribute to a justification, continues to apply. The *Model Penal Code* in the United States requires an actor to have believed that his act was necessary before that act can be described as justified (American Law Institute 1985, Article 3, Section 3.02). A plea of self-defence in England and Wales cannot succeed unless, in addition to being in danger, the defendant realised that this was the case (see Smith and Hogan 1996, pp.259–270). While the situation in Anglo-American law is at variance with the suggestion of Williams, it is consistent with the view of Fletcher (1978, pp.555–566) that information unknown to the actor cannot justify his act.

Psychiatric aspects of justification

To what extent can psychiatric factors be expected to provide justifications for acts which would otherwise be considered criminal? They clearly cannot be relevant to the first aspect of justification described here, that which relates to the objective rightness or wrongness of what was done. Even where the second approach, that which examines the defendant's reasons for doing as he did, is adopted, the extension of the definition to include some mistakes seems to allow little room for psychiatric factors to operate. The mistakes, if they are to contribute to a justification, are required to be reasonable.

What is reasonable? Wilkie, discussing the partial defence of provocation, identified three possibilities (see *State* v. *Hoyt* at 654). The first was statistical. 'Reasonable' was what most people would do. The second was moral. 'Reasonable' was what the law thought people should do. Wilkie's preferred definition, however, hinged on the ability of the jury to empathise with the defendant. Reasonable feelings or conduct, as opposed to unreasonable feelings or conduct, could be 'understood sympathetically'.

Mental disorders represent statistical deviations from the norm. They do not usually lead their sufferers to behave in a morally praiseworthy fashion. Wilkie's first two definitions of reasonableness would therefore seem to exclude the consequences of mental disorders. With regard to the third, juries might be able to understand sympathetically the motives of a defendant whose mistake was the result of psychiatric disorder, particularly if psychiatrists were able to give evidence to explain the effects of that disorder. Psychiatric evidence is usually excluded, however, unless a mental-state defence, such as insanity or diminished responsibility, is being put forward.[24] It seems that most psychiatric mistakes, and certainly those which lead to inappropriate self-defence, would not be regarded by the law as reasonable.[25]

EXCUSE
General and legal definitions

Austin's (1956–57) essence of an excuse is that it is in some way inadequate, in describing the excused action 'X', to say that A did X. It may be that it was not, in the normal sense, A that did it. The physical force driving the action may have stemmed from someone else.[26] Equally, someone else may have provided the motive for the action, as would be the case if A had acted with a gun at his back. It may also be that it is inappropriate to use the word 'did' to describe A's relationship to the action. It may have been an accident or he may have slipped. Finally, we may cavil at saying that X was what he did. He may have thought, quite reasonably, that he was doing something else. If someone happens to step in front of a photographer's viewfinder while walking to work, it seems wrong to describe his action as one of ruining a carefully composed photograph. The photograph may have been ruined, but A was doing something else. In the view of Austin, we claim an excuse when we accept that an action was bad but do not accept responsibility.

What of excuses as they relate to the criminal law? Hart has offered a general definition:

> The individual is not liable to punishment if at the time of his doing what would otherwise be a punishable act he was unconscious, mistaken about the physical

consequences of his bodily movements or the nature or qualities of the thing or persons affected by them, or, in some cases, if he was subjected to threats or other gross forms of coercion or was the victim of certain types of mental disease. (Hart 1968, p.28)

Hart's analysis is reflected in the excuses which are recognised in Anglo-American law. Unconscious acts are automatisms. Mistakes, as discussed earlier, are allowed to exculpate when they remove *mens rea*. Successful pleas of duress can lead to acquittal[27] and, in the case of homicide in England and Wales, provocation can lead to a conviction for manslaughter instead of murder. Mental disease is catered for by the insanity defence, and mental abnormality by the doctrine of diminished responsibility.

The definitions of excuse offered by lawyers are similar to those suggested by Austin and Hart. Williams (1982) claims that an excuse either denies intent, recklessness or negligence on the part of the defendant, or affirms that he was not acting as a fully free and responsible agent. This definition is similar to that provided by the Tuscan Penal Code of the last century, which allowed the acquittal of a mentally abnormal defendant when his condition denied him full awareness of what he was doing or deprived him of his free will (see Guarnieri 1993, p.110). Williams goes on to point out that an excused act may be resisted by the person against whom it is directed.[28] In addition, excuses are personal (Fletcher 1978, pp.641–644, 762; Williams 1982, pp.735, 736). Someone assisting an excused actor cannot benefit from the excuse of his partner and needs one of his own if he is to avoid conviction.[29] Mistaken information, according to Williams (1982, p.740), cannot justify but can excuse.

All definitions, however, depend to some extent on the views of the 'definer' as to the purpose of the criminal justice system. It is only by reference to this that we can establish who is to be absolved from criminal liability. A retributivist will wish to excuse those who do not deserve punishment, while a utilitarian will be disinclined to punish where punishment would not serve the common good. The next section will review three theories of excuse. The first of these depends on a predominantly utilitarian approach to criminal justice. The other two are more retributive in their origins and have been named here, following Moore (1990), the choice and character theories of excuse. The means by which psychiatric factors affect the process of excusing will then be examined.

Types of excuses

Utilitarian theories

A utilitarian approach to criminal justice requires the greatest good for the greatest number. Its most famous exponent was Jeremy Bentham (1823). His theory of punishment is described by Hart (1968, p.40) as an 'economy of threats'. Bentham regarded responsibility as a condition to be satisfied if the threat to punish, announced by the criminal law, was to have the maximum effect. There were two situations in which the imposition of criminal sanctions would fail to serve utilitarian aims. First, the individual might, for instance as a result of infancy or insanity, be unamenable to logical persuasion. Second, even if he was so amenable, his circumstances might be such as to give him no choice as to his course of action. In these two situations, punishment would be pointless because others would not be deterred. Bentham would thus ensure the maintenance of law at the lowest cost in pain.

It is not clear how, if these suggestions were adopted, the economy of threats would be regulated. Bentham would have to find a common currency for, and a reliable measurement of, the suffering endured by the convicted man and the suffering avoided by those who would become victims were he not punished. In addition, Hart (1968, p.43) pointed out, a system run on purely utilitarian principles might punish defendants who would currently be excused. Some people who commit prohibited acts see themselves as having a chance of claiming duress, self-defence or provocation. They would best be deterred by a system which did not recognise these defences. Others might take more precautions against making a mistake or against being involved in an accident if punishment was inflicted without reference to the actor's state of mind when he acted.

Bentham's arguments offer no reason not to punish the duressed or provoked, or indeed those who act while mistaken as to the circumstances or by accident, if the harm of punishment is outweighed by other good. In the normal sense of the word, in fact, it is doubtful whether Bentham is talking about excuses at all. Excuses, as Fletcher and Williams pointed out, are personal (see p.29). To Bentham, the criminal's mental condition is relevant not because it may stop us from holding him responsible for what he has done, but because by taking it into account we can render the criminal law more effective.

To Hart, this was not adequate. 'More is at stake,' he wrote, 'than the single principle of maintaining the laws at their most efficacious level' (Hart 1968, p.44). Hart argued that we have a 'moral preference for a legal system that requires mental conditions of responsibility over a system of total strict liability' (Hart 1968, p.44). We are prepared to sacrifice the possible benefits of a system of strict liability in order that we can require, before conviction, a defendant to be responsible for his act or omission. Excuses, Hart argued, prevent the attribution of this responsibility (Hart 1968, p.31). How do they do this?

Choice theory

The second theory of blame and excuse is often attributed to Kant (1788, p.66). The basis of the theory was described by Blackstone (1769). All excuses could be 'reduced to this single consideration, the want or defect of will. An involuntary act, as it has no claim to merit, so neither can it induce any guilt: the concurrence of the will, when it has the choice either to do or avoid the act in question, being the only thing which renders human actions praiseworthy or culpable' (p.20).

Hart developed the theme in this century, arguing that individuals are only responsible for what they do when they have the capacity and opportunity to do otherwise (Hart 1968, p.152). He offered two justifications for this. The first was utilitarian.[30] Basing excuses on lack of choice maximised two competing priorities – individual freedom and crime prevention. The second was that fairness and justice demanded some such arrangement, whatever utilitarian balance was being sought (Hart 1968; see also Moore 1990, p.33).

What do capacity and opportunity mean in this context? When choice theorists such as Hart (1968) and Moore (1990) refer to capacity they usually have in mind internal factors. When they refer to opportunity they have in mind an absence of external constraint. Lack of either capacity or opportunity is enough to excuse. As Gross (1979, p.137) points out, however, choice theory cannot establish which should be more important to a defence. In addition, several qualifications have to be applied to choice theory as described here if it is to describe our usual practices of excusing.

The first concerns opportunity. What of someone who places himself in a situation where his opportunity to operate within the confines of the law is limited or precluded? Should he be treated in the same way as someone whose lack of opportunity arises through no fault of their own? The English courts have held not. When the defendant had joined a gang which he knew might put pressure on him to commit an offence, he was not able to use the defence of duress when he committed an offence as a result of that pressure (see *R. v. Sharp*). Moore refers to 'fair opportunity' (1990, p.40), whereby the lack of opportunity, if it is to contribute to an excuse, must have arisen through no fault of the actor.

A second qualification concerns capacity. Is my unprovoked assault excused by my dislike of my victim? No. Is my violent outburst excused if, throughout my life, I have demonstrated an inability to appreciate the feelings of others? Unlikely. Would the same outburst be excused if my personality had changed recently following a blow to the head? More likely. The choice theorist has to distinguish lack of capacity from an unwillingness to apply that capacity.

The final qualification to choice theory stems from the fact that even if their actions are excused, people still make choices to engage in those actions. People under duress, it could be argued, choose to yield. Mentally disordered defendants, even those who exhibit delusions and hallucinations, still choose to do some things and not to do others (see Duff 1993, p.352). If choice theory is to make allowance for such cases, a distinction has to be made, for the purposes of attributing responsibility, between choices which will be deemed 'adequate' or 'proper' and those which will not.

Character theory

The third approach to excuses derives from the work of Hume (1748, see especially pp.154–156). In this approach a central position is given to the character of the actor. When Aristotle referred to character in the context of responsibility, he was restricting his use of the term to those traits over which an individual can exert voluntary control. Character theorists of excuse do not mean this, however. They are referring to any durable personal characteristic, whether or not it is susceptible to the will.

Fletcher (1978, p.799) put the essence of the theory succinctly. An excuse 'precludes an inference from the act to the actor's character'. My sexually inappropriate behaviour is excused by my mental illness because the illness somehow comes between the act and any conclusion regarding my character. The law punishes intentional killing more severely than reckless killing, Bayles (1982) argues, because the character which can be inferred from the act of intentional killing is more malign. Since this way of looking at excuses dispenses with any requirement to prove that an act was voluntary, it avoids the debate as to whether our actions are determined or the result of free will.[31] Incorporated into a system of criminal law, however, it would allow the court's assessment of a defendant's character and, in particular, the court's conclusion that the prohibited act did not reflect that character, to excuse.

The criminal law limits the circumstances under which personal characteristics can exculpate (Fletcher 1978, p.513). Before the partial defence of provocation is allowed, for instance, the law requires not only that the defendant lost control but also that a reasonable man would have done the same (see the discussion of provocation in Chapter 3). An objective standard is being added to a subjective one.[32] The law does this, according to Fletcher, because of a fear that if the choices which a defendant made can be explained in terms of his physical or psychological characteristics, the scope for attributing blame will reduce. He quotes a French proverb, 'Tout comprendre, c'est tout pardonner'.[33]

Fletcher implies that this is a reason to prefer character theory to choice theory. Is it? It was argued in Chapter 1 that an acceptance of the principles of determinism would inevitably lead to the abandonment of the concept of responsibility for a criminal act. It may be this which concerns the French. It was also argued in Chapter 1, however, that for reasons which relate to our desire to predict and control what will happen to us, we will continue to require responsibility as a condition for punishment. If we continue to require responsibility, we will continue to allow excuses. In deciding who to excuse, we have the option of choice theory or character theory. The possibility that to explain all is to excuse all poses problems at least as profound for Fletcher's preferred alternative, character theory, as those it poses for choice theory.

If we are required to use choice theory to say whether a defendant should be excused, we may change our minds as more information becomes available. Our initial assumption is usually that someone's capacity to choose is normal; this is the position taken by the courts. As we become more aware of their intellectual and emotional characteristics, we may start to wonder whether our initial assumption was correct. To this extent, the more we understand why a crime was committed the more likely we will be to excuse. Aranella (1990) has criticised choice theory on these grounds, arguing that the provision of an excuse is rendered dependent on our ability to empathise.

In some cases, however, as we learn more about an individual and the circumstances of his offence we become more, not less, convinced that he made an adequate choice to act as he did. We are inclined to excuse someone who acted violently when subjected to verbal abuse which would have provoked a violent response in most people. When we find out that the individual concerned was prevented by deafness from hearing this abuse, or by his personality from being moved by it, we are less likely to excuse. The alternative to choice theory offered by Aranella, Bayles and Fletcher – excusing where an act fails to reflect the character of the actor – does not avoid the possibility that our willingness to excuse is dependent on our level of understanding. In character theory, it could be argued, to explain all is to forgive nothing. If a person's lawbreaking behaviour is understandable in terms of their previous personality, they can have no excuse because their act will no longer be 'out of character'.

Several other difficulties attend the character theory of excuse, difficulties which do not arise if choice theory is adopted. First, where a 'bad' person, as judged from aspects of their behaviour which do not transgress legal norms, has so far failed to break the law, the character theorist could punish anyway. Fletcher's defence of character theory on this point invokes utilitarian principles, 'We accept the artificiality of inferring character from a single deed as the price of maintaining the suspect's privacy' (Fletcher 1978, p.800). Other defenders of character theory have pointed out that their scheme identifies only necessary, and not sufficient, conditions for punishment. Different principles can then be invoked to decide when this punishment should be applied.

Second, what of the man with an exemplary past who commits an atrocious crime? Should not all acts which are 'out of character' be excused? No, says Fletcher, only those acts which exhibit traits which are outside the actor's control (Fletcher 1978, p.514). Greed, for instance, should not count. But to resort to control as a criterion is to end up in the same boat as choice theory, having to decide which of our actions are truly under such control. The third problem concerns the point at which an offence can no longer be said to reflect the character of an actor. If a rapist turns out to have no record of sexual violence but to have conducted a large number of assaults, can he argue that his offence is out of character? Finally, what of cases where no motivation for the crime can be divined? Are these crimes 'in' character or 'out' of it?

It may be that the failure of an act to reflect the character of the actor is better seen as a reason to suspect that an excuse exists than as itself providing an excuse.[34] When the schoolteacher hits a child for no apparent reason, we might raise an eyebrow and comment that such behaviour 'is not like him'. Only when it transpires that the teacher was a diabetic whose insulin had been incorrectly prescribed do we nod and preface, 'It's not like him' with, 'I thought he must have been unwell.' The fact that the act was out of character has made us wonder, not made us excuse. When we act under excusing conditions such as insanity or duress we may act in ways which are 'out of character'. But this does not mean that all acts which are out of character should be excused.

Psychiatric aspects of excuse

In contrast to the situation as pertains to justification, where, it was suggested, the role of psychiatric factors is limited, psychiatric factors can excuse. Even if a strictly utilitarian, or Benthamite, approach is adopted, the mental state of the actor is important in determining his ability to be deterred and the degree to which punishing him is likely to deter others. Bentham's way of looking at excuses, however, poses several problems. It is not clear how the calculation of the greatest good for the greatest number is to be made. Perhaps more importantly, exemption from punishment on purely utilitarian grounds fails to reflect our preference for a criminal justice system which requires for conviction the attribution of responsibility.

Those theories of excuse which do reflect this preference, theories which have been labelled here 'choice theory' and 'character theory', also allow the application of psychiatric factors. Choice theory requires the capacity and fair opportunity to act otherwise before responsibility is said to be present. Most authors use capacity to refer to internal factors and opportunity to refer to external circumstances. The choice which an individual makes as to his course of action may be different in the presence of symptoms such as cognitive impairment, abnormal beliefs and hallucinations. The information on which the decision is based may have been tampered with or his capacity for self-control reduced (the psychiatric conditions which can contribute to excuses are discussed in Chapter 4).

The relevance of psychiatric factors to the character theory of excuse is that mental disorders frequently affect the long-standing traits which we refer to as aspects of someone's personality. Indeed, in recognising the behavioural signs of mental illness relatives and friends frequently refer to someone's actions as 'out of character'. But the shortcomings of the character theory of excuse, discussed earlier, are particularly evident with respect to psychiatric considerations. Two specific problems arise.

First, while it is safe to say that an action was 'out of character' once an excusing condition has been established, the reverse does not apply. The courts have never accepted that an act being out of character is, on its own, sufficient to excuse the actor on psychiatric grounds. Psychiatric excuses require, in addition, that some form of mental disorder be present (the various psychiatric excuses in the criminal law are described in Chapter 5). Second, many mental-state abnormalities are present from birth or, at least, from before the point at which someone's character can be said to have become established. This is the case in mental handicap and, in many cases, for the group of conditions known as personality disorders. The issue of whether or not these conditions excuse antisocial behaviour is, as will be seen in the ensuing chapters, the subject of debate. It is difficult to see how the character theory of excuse can inform this debate. If the behavioural and emotional traits which a person evinces do not comprise that person's character, it is difficult to see what does. And if the person's criminal acts are consistent with that character, the character theorist cannot excuse.

SUMMARY

Legal usage of the term 'justification' has been inconsistent. On the one hand, particularly when defined by jurisprudential theorists, it has been used to refer to an objective 'rightness' or 'wrongness', irrespective of what the author of an action thought he was doing. On the other, particularly when the term is used by judges in appellate decisions but also when described in relation to self-defence in the *Model Penal Code* (American Law Institute 1985), it includes consideration of the actor's subjective condition. It has been argued here that this lack of consistency in the law reflects common usage. We use the term 'justification' to refer both to the rights and wrongs of a particular deed, and to the adequacy of someone's reasons for acting as they did.

With regard to excuse, the meaning of the term is uncontroversial: excuses reduce the extent to which we attribute responsibility for an action to an actor. What has been the subject of debate, however, is the grounds on which we do so. Utilitarian excuses, if they exist at all, address the issue of whether and when we can be said to be responsible only to the extent that such calculations affect the greater good. Character theory comes closer to describing the process by which, in some circumstances, we refuse to attribute responsibility. Character theory has several drawbacks, however, not least that it begs the question of whether an act which we would normally use to weigh the actor's character can or cannot be used in this way on this occasion.

The best explanation of why some people have excuses is that something has interfered with the person's ability to choose. Psychiatric factors seem likely to influence this ability to the extent that they render the actor's choice different in some way from that which would be regarded as normal for him or normal for other people. By contrast, psychiatric factors are unlikely to influence the process of justification, a process which requires an objective assessment of right or wrong or that any mistakes made by the actor be reasonable. To the extent that psychiatric factors exculpate, they do so by excusing. The ways in which they do so will be examined in Chapter 4.

NOTES

1. In England and Wales there is a time limit of six months for the prosecution of summary offences and of one year for engaging in sexual intercourse with a girl under the age of 16 (see Richardson 1999, ss.1.200, 20.79). Other countries have statutes of limitations which apply more widely, usually with exceptions for 'crimes against humanity'.

2. For further criticism of the practice of making a distinction see Kadish 1987, p.259.

3. Some authors regard voluntariness as part of *mens rea* (Radzinowicz and Turner 1945, pp.195–261; Turner 1966, pp.26–31). The majority, however, regard it as part of the *actus reus* (Allen 1997, p.21; Ashworth 1975, p.102; Clarkson and Keating 1998, p.96; Patient 1968; Richardson 1999, s.17.21; Williams 1961, p.12).

4. Denying *mens rea* is one of the few ways in which a mistake can form the basis of a successful defence. The example given by Smith and Hogan (1996) is that of importing a crate believing it to contain non-dutiable items when, in fact, it contains whisky (p.222). A mistake as to what the law forbids, however, is no excuse when it does not deny *mens rea*. One still intended to import whisky (see also Richardson 1999, s.17.11).

5. Duress, however, does not excuse in the case of murder. The House of Lords has confirmed that in England and Wales the defendant is expected to sacrifice his own life rather than take that of another (see *R. v. Howe*).

6. Writers in jurisprudence are equivocal as to whether a successful defence denies the criminality of an act. Smith and Hogan (1996, p.194) surround the term 'unlawful' with inverted commas when using it to describe excused acts. Williams, describing an attack by an excusable person, states: 'In a sense the attack is non-criminal and may even be lawful' (1982, p.732). He is less guarded elsewhere (1983, p.39), arguing that 'the *actus reus* is the whole external situation forbidden by law, and one cannot properly depict that situation without mentioning that no defence must exist'. By this argument, all excuses which result in a successful defence should presumably be regarded as denying criminality.

7. Fletcher (1979, pp.1358, 1359); see also Eser (1976): justification requires the 'balancing of all values involved' (p.635); Yeo (1990): 'if the actor's conduct causes less harm than the harm which he or she thereby avoids, the conduct is justifiable' (p.6).

8. Uniacke's 'agent-perspectival' justification is not entirely subjective, however. She specifically excludes acts consequent upon an unreasonable mistake.

9. The law has been similarly unwilling to allow unreasonable mistakes to contribute to a justification: 'Through mistaken beliefs that are unreasonable will always serve in this way to excuse, they will usually be rejected when the defense seeks to justify, rather than excuse, what was done' (Gross 1979, p.264).

10. For a similar view to that of Gordon see Smith (1989, p.10), who implies that justification addresses whether or not an illegal act, or tort, has taken place. Later in his series of lectures, however, Smith says that justification is to be defined on moral grounds (p.13) and, still later, on the basis of 'social value' (p.53).

11. Exculpatory defences deny that one was responsible for a criminal act. Non-exculpatory defences, such as 'out of time' and prior conviction for the offence, offer no such denial (see Williams 1982, and the discussion at the beginning of this chapter).

12. Necessity may also be a defence to a charge of dangerous driving under the Road Traffic Act 1988 (see *R. v. Backshall, R. v. Symonds*).

13. See also the use of the phrase in *R*. v. *Conway* (at 290) and *R*. v. *Martin* (at 652). The principles stated in Martin were confirmed by the Divisional Court in *DPP* v. *Rogers*. Williams (1982, p.742) refers to 'compulsion of circumstances'.

14. Glazebrook (1972, p.93) thinks that unless a statute expressly prevents them from doing so, the courts hold that statutory provision is not intended to apply in cases where more harm would result from the defendant obeying the law than breaking it.

15. See Fletcher (1974, p.1282); also Glazebrook (1972) for a more wide-ranging discussion of the role of necessity in English criminal law. Glazebrook shares Fletcher's view that the defence hinges on showing that the least harmful course was adopted (see his p.88).

16. *US* v. *Holmes*, although the court implied (at 367) that the killing would have been legal had lots been drawn to decide who would do the throwing.

17. See also Lord Hailsham's view that the defence of necessity operates according to objective criteria in *R*. v. *Howe*, at 429.

18. Plus a small amount of harm to the cause of deterring other motorists from driving on the pavement. Presumably this is a trivial consideration given that most motorists would realise that Willer's defence would not be available to them.

19. See Cohen (1977) for an analysis of why juries' judgements of probability cannot be explained in purely statistical terms.

20. There is, therefore, a subjective requirement that the actor believe his action is necessary. The criterion by which the presence or absence of justification is to be judged, however, is objective. The Code requires that 'the harm or evil sought to be avoided be greater than that which would be caused by the commission of the offense, not that the defendant believe it to be so' (American Law Institute 1985, p.12). This definition of justification is a variance with that used in the discussion of self-defence, when the Code holds that mistaken beliefs can justify (see Article 3, Section 3.04).

21. The law's approach is not entirely subjective, however. A person may only use such force as is (objectively) reasonable in the circumstances as he (subjectively) believes them to be (see *R*. v. *Owino*).

22. As has been acknowledged by the courts of England and Wales. See Lord Morris in *R*. v. *Palmer* at 1088: 'A person defending himself cannot weigh to a nicety the exact measure of his necessary defensive action.' Lord Morris went on to say that the defendant should need to show only that he did what he 'honestly and instinctively thought' was necessary.

23. Although the law does not require someone who is defending himself to measure precisely the minimum amount of force required, there does come a point where the force used will be deemed excessive. At this point the defence ceases to be available (see *R*. v. *Clegg*).

24. In *R*. v. *Turner* [1975] Q.B. 834 the Court of Appeal held that psychiatric testimony should be excluded where the evidence related only to ordinary human experience. L.J. Lawton commented (at 841): 'Jurors do not need psychiatrists to tell them how ordinary folk who are not suffering from any mental illness are likely to react to the stresses and strains of life.' In practice, the courts may be willing to admit expert evidence in more cases than this would suggest, provided that evidence is within the field of expertise of the witness, is likely to help the court and defers to the values and objectives of the law (Roberts 1996; see also Beaumont 1988, Mackay and Colman 1996).

25. Some go as far as to argue that 'unreason', or irrationality, is the hallmark of mental disorder (see Chapter 6).

26. 'If there be an actual forcing of a man, as if A by force take the arm of B and the weapon in his hand and therewith stabs C whereof he dies, this is murder in A but B is not guilty' (Hale 1736, p.434).

27. Except when the charge is murder.

28. In contrast to a justified one (see p.26; see also Fletcher 1978, pp.760, 761; Williams 1982, p.732).

29. Diminished responsibility, for instance, is only available to the person who suffers from the abnormality of mind.

30. Despite his reservations concerning Bentham's 'economy of threats', Hart was not hostile to utilitarian considerations. In *Punishment and Responsibility*, he refers to 'the middle way, which I myself have attempted to tread, between a purely forward-looking scheme of social hygiene and theories which treat retribution as a general justifying aim' (1968, p.233).

31. Critics of character theory concede this point. See Moore (1990, p.50): '[The character theorist's] idea of responsibility does not depend on an actor's choices being free.'

32. Oliver Wendell Holmes wrote that the standards of the criminal law 'require [a person] ... at his own peril to come up to a certain height. They take no account of incapacities, unless the weakness is so marked as to fall into well known exceptions, such as infancy or madness' (Holmes 1881, pp.50–51).

33. Ferracuti (1996) traces 'to understand all is to forgive all' to the nineteenth-century German philosopher and physiologist, Moleschott.

34. See, for instance, Sullivan's (1996) argument that a woman's premenstrual tension should lead to acquittal if the incident was 'untypical of them', but only if she acted in a state of 'destabilisation but for which the agent would not have done what she did'.

CHAPTER 3

Psychiatric Aspects of Mitigation

The Latin verb *mitigare* means 'to make more gentle'. There are two reasons to mitigate legal sanctions. The first is that a law is seen as too severe. Juries in the eighteenth century, required to establish the amount of money which had been stolen in the course of a robbery, frequently set the figure just below that required for the imposition of the death penalty. The practice was described at the time as 'pious perjury' (Blackstone 1769, p.239). Romilly (1810, p.66) observed that judges reduced sentences for the same reason. The second reason to reduce the sentence of a convicted offender is to obtain a better fit between the punishment on the one hand, and the individual and the circumstances of his offence on the other. Eighteenth-century judges were permitted to substitute transportation for the death penalty where they considered it 'reasonable upon the circumstances of the case'.[1] This is the sense in which the term 'mitigation' will be used here.

Anglo-American criminal law traditionally left to the judge or magistrate the decision whether to mitigate (Thomas 1978, 1979a). In nineteenth-century England this judicial discretion faced two challenges. The first stemmed from Bentham and his followers, who argued for the codification of the common law.[2] The second was a less ambitious but more successful attempt by Robert Peel to consolidate some of the 750 statutes which by the early part of the century defined criminal behaviour (Radzinowicz 1948, pp.574–577). Even in the second half of the nineteenth century, however, the penalty in many non-capital felony cases was at the discretion of the judge and lay between one day in prison and a lifetime of penal servitude (Thomas 1978, p.37; 1979a, p.1).[3]

In England and Wales during the second half of the twentieth century the discretion granted to judges and magistrates has been restricted, and the criteria by which sentences are mitigated have become more visible. The Court of Appeal has passed down 'guideline judgements' in which the factors which should mitigate the sentence for various crimes are stated (see *R.* v. *Willis* on buggery; also Ashworth 1995b, pp.27–30). The Criminal Justice Act 1991 provided what were described as the most detailed provisions on sentencing of any English statute this century (Ashworth 1992, p.xxi), only for it to be followed by the Criminal Justice Act 1993 and the Public Order Act 1994. Finally, the sentencing decisions of the Court of Appeal are now reported in detail.

These changes notwithstanding, several difficulties attend any examination of the principles by which sentences are mitigated. First, there is a tradition of inconsistency in the sentencing decisions of the Court of Appeal.[4] Thus the judge or magistrate is required to take into account any physical disability or illness which would subject the offender to an unusual degree of hardship if he was imprisoned (*B.* v. *Herasymenko* [1975], quoted in Thomas 1979b, p.216) but an offender's individual reaction to prison life should not affect the sentence (*R.* v. *Kay*). Second, the degree to which appellate decisions apply in magistrates' courts, where most sentencing takes place, is uncertain (see Wasik and Pease 1987, p.2). Third, factors which reduce the sentence for one crime may not do the same for another. Mitigation may be withheld if the crime is regarded as serious. Lord Justice Lawton, sitting in judgement on a series of armed bank robberies, stated: '...the fact that a man has not much of a criminal record, if any at all, is not a powerful factor to be taken into consideration when the court is dealing with cases of this gravity' (*R.* v. *Turner* [1975] 61 Cr.App.R. 67 at 91). Thomas considers judges less likely to mitigate if, when they pass sentence, they have in mind public protection or deterrence (Thomas 1979b, p.47).[5]

Fourth, factors which usually lead to mitigation of sentence occasionally change the category of the offence. A system of criminal justice could have one offence of robbery and treat the use of a gun as an aggravating factor, or it could treat robbery and armed robbery as separate crimes (Ashworth 1995b, p.129). In England and Wales the fact that the defendant was provoked usually goes to mitigation, but in cases of homicide it has the effect of reducing what would otherwise be a murder conviction to one of manslaughter.[6] Finally, the mechanism by which mitigation occurs varies from one criminal justice system to another. This chapter will discuss the psychiatric aspects of mitigation in England and Wales. Similar principles operate in the United States (see Hall, George and Force 1976).

What of aggravating factors? Are these simply the opposite of mitigating ones? Racial motivation is regarded as an aggravating factor in cases of assault in England and Wales, but the absence of such motivation would not normally be described as mitigating. Sentencing guidelines require what Ashworth (1995b, p.129) has called a 'neutral' value, from which mitigation subtracts and to which aggravation adds. To an offender, however, it matters little whether past mis-demeanours are said to result in aggravation or loss of mitigation. Some aggravating factors, such as premeditation, are no more than the negative form of mitigating factors, such as impulsivity. This chapter will discuss the psychiatric aspects of all factors which affect the sentence for a given offence.

The general principles which affect mitigation at the sentencing stage will be discussed first. As discussed above, however, some mitigating factors operate to alter the category of the conviction. Two of these – provocation and diminished responsibility on grounds of mental abnormality – will be discussed in the second and third sections.[7] The offence of infanticide, like the doctrine of diminished responsibility, allows some defendants who have killed to avoid the mandatory life sentence for murder. Unlike diminished responsibility, however, it can be charged by the Crown in the first instance and will be dealt with in Chapter 5.

GENERAL PRINCIPLES GOING TO MITIGATION
The circumstances of the offence

Three types of factor, relating to the circumstances of the offence, influence sentencing. First, the level of harm done is relevant. If a minimal amount of damage is caused (for instance, in the course of a burglary), this is allowed to mitigate (*R. v. Mussell* at 612); burglaries conducted while the occupants are at home are likely to receive stiffer sentences (*R. v. Mussell* at 612), presumably because the risk of confrontation is greater. Second, the quality of the act is important. Thus an offence committed against a public official may be punished especially harshly (*R. v. Nawrot* at 240), as may a crime which involves a breach of trust (*R. v. Dawson* at 250). The involvement of a number of people simultaneously (*R. v. Rogers-Hinks* at 237) and the presence of racial motivation (*R. v. Alderson* at 302) have similarly aggravating effects. Offenders whose victims are especially vulnerable through being old (*R. v. Allen and Bennett* at 467) or young (*R. v. Boswell* at 317) are liable to longer sentences.

Third, there are considerations which relate to the defendant's state of mind when he acted. Impulsive acts receive lighter sentences than premeditated ones (Ashworth 1995b, p.134).[8] Sentences for fraud are mitigated where the act was one of omission rather than deception (*R. v. Stewart* at 143). Young offenders can expect to receive shorter sentences than older ones.[9] Entrapment by the police can mitigate,[10] as can the defendant's having been under stress at the time the offence was committed (*R. v. Jeffrey* at 266; also Thomas 1979b, p.207). An element of self-defence in the defendant's actions can have the same effect.[11] Finally, a defendant who played only a small role in the crime can expect to be treated more leniently than can the ringleader (*R. v. Rogers-Hinks* at 237).

What principles are operating when factors relating to the level of harm and to the quality of the act are allowed to influence sentencing? According to Ashworth, in taking into account the quality of the act, the courts are simply establishing another measure of the level of harm. Thus, he argues, a racially motivated attack is punished more severely because, in addition to meeting the definition of assault, it 'constitutes a further infringement of the victim's rights, as protected by the laws against racial discrimination' (Ashworth 1995b, p.130).[12] Attacks conducted by two or more people induce more fear and helplessness in the victim (Ashworth 1995b, p.130) and offences carried out against public officials or in breach of trust are either of greater 'social significance' or more 'socially harmful' (Ashworth 1995b, pp.132, 131). This is true, but may not always be what the courts have in mind when they pass sentence. In the case of one assault on a public official, the court was clearly bent not upon measuring the level of harm but upon preventing repetition: 'It seems that deterrent sentences are necessary' (R. v. Nawrot at 240). Similar considerations seem to have applied in the breach of trust case mentioned above, where the Court of Appeal stated that such cases undermine public confidence: 'The matters of financial dealing with which this man was involved cannot be carried out unless confidence is reposed in those who carry out these transactions on behalf of members of the public' (R. v. Dawson at 250).

With regard to those mitigating factors which bear on the third aspect of the circumstances of the offence, the defendant's state of mind when he acted, the principles at work resemble those of justification and excuse. Acting in self-defence is a justification and an excuse (see the discussion in Chapter 2). Where the level of violence exceeds that permitted, and a prosecution for assault takes place, the element of self-defence may still be grounds for mitigation.[13] Being a child is an excuse.[14] When a young offender is punished less severely, it may be because his age approaches that at which he would not be punished at all.[15] Mitigation in response to an impulsive act, police entrapment or stress may also be the result of the defendant being seen as less responsible. His ability to choose was impaired (or, if the character theory of excuse is preferred, one can extrapolate less reliably from the act to the offender's character).

What is the relevance of psychiatry to these mitigating factors relating to the circumstances of the offence? With regard to the level of harm done, psychiatry has little to say. Although the level of lasting psychological damage, consequent upon an assault, varies greatly from one victim to another, the criminal law has traditionally concerned itself with the level of physical harm done. Only recently has mental harm been included within the definition of offences such as actual bodily harm (R. v. Burstow; R. v. Chan-Fook; R. v. Ireland; R. v. Morris). With regard to those grounds for mitigation which relate to the nature of the act, it seems equally unlikely that psychiatric factors will be of relevance. Although one of the principles at work is deterrence, it seems that it is the effect of the sentence on the public, and not its influence on the offender, which judges consider.[16]

With respect to the defendant's state of mind when he acted, however, psychiatric factors do seem to be of relevance. Shapland (1981, p.65) found that a psychiatric illness was one of the characteristics commonly mentioned in speeches made in support of mitigation. Psychiatric disposals in the form of probation orders with conditions of treatment and hospital orders may reflect a desire on the part of the courts to mitigate the sentences of mentally disordered offenders.[17] The courts do not always hear psychiatric evidence, however, and may exclude it when it is offered as part of a defence other than insanity, sane automatism or diminished responsibility (see p.32; also *R. v. Clarke*).

One condition which affects the defendant's state of mind but which does not usually go to mitigation is intoxication (although for crimes requiring proof of specific intent, intoxication may negate that intent: see Clarkson and Keating 1998, pp.405–436; Richardson 1999, ss.17.105–17.112). Thomas quotes the case of a young man with no previous convictions who set fire to the house of a former employer. Although the court took the view that the offence had been committed because the appellant had had too much to drink, it refused to mitigate.[18] The reason given by Ashworth (1983, p.173) for such decisions is that the mitigating effects of weakened self-control and lack of appreciation of the circumstances are balanced by social considerations regarding the use of intoxicants. This implies that successive instances of drunken offending should be treated similarly. A first drunken offence, however, seems more excusable than a second. Once someone knows what they are capable of doing when intoxicated, it is reasonable to expect them to take more care. The Committee on Mentally Abnormal Offenders (1975, pp.236–237) recommended a new offence of 'dangerous intoxication' with a maximum sentence which increased from 12 months imprisonment for a first offence to three years for a subsequent one. In contrast to their attitude to intoxication, the courts have been more sympathetic to defendants who are alcoholics (Thomas 1979b, p.210), unless they have previously failed to cooperate with treatment (Thomas 1979b, p.211).

Consideration for dependants

It is rare for a defendant's sentence to be reduced because his family will suffer (Thomas 1979b, p.211). In certain instances, however, the courts seem to be influenced by an unwillingness to cause unnecessary harm to others.[19] Thus the presence at home of young children (*R. v. Vaughan*) and the life-threatening illness of a family member (*R. v. Haleth*) have both led to sentences being reduced. At least in the view of some defence counsel, the fact that the wife of the accused is expecting a baby soon after the trial can influence the judge, as can the requirements of childcare (see Shapland 1981, p.65). Thomas has identified three areas where, in contrast to the general rule, the likely effect of the sentence upon the defendant's family is allowed to mitigate. These are: where the hardship which will be experienced by the family is excessive; where the mother of young children commits a crime which is not serious; and where there is the prospect of both parents being imprisoned simultaneously (Thomas 1979b, pp.211–213).

Factors relating to the individual offender

Two groups of considerations relate to the offender himself. The first concerns his character. In some instances, the courts take into account those aspects of this character which can be inferred from the circumstances surrounding his being apprehended and tried. Thus those who own up before being discovered are likely to receive a more lenient sentence (*R.* v. *Whybrew; R.* v. *Wigley*) as are those who inform on their partners in crime (*R.* v. *Lowe*). Those who plead guilty can expect a 'discount' of 20 per cent of their sentence, on average (Moxon 1988, p.32). Judges may have in mind the benefits to society, in terms of apprehending other lawbreakers, of providing an incentive for cooperation. And other good may come of a guilty plea, such as preventing witnesses from having to go through the ordeal of giving evidence (*R.* v. *Billam* at 350). It is also likely, however, that judges regard defendants of good character as less in need of deterrence[20] and as better candidates for rehabilitation.[21]

The courts also take into account aspects of a defendant's character, such as the nature and number of his previous convictions, which are unrelated to the offence. Attempts to stay out of trouble can be considered (see *R.* v. *Canham* [1975], quoted in Thomas 1979b, p.201). Walker (1991, p.98) has observed that dramatic behaviour influences courts more than unobtrusive decency. On one occasion a sentence for fraud was reduced because the culprit was to receive an award from the Royal Humane Society for diving into a river to rescue a drowning boy (*R.* v. *Keightley*), and in another case the fact that the accused was known to have tried to rescue some children from a blazing house was taken into consideration (*R.* v. *Reid* [1982] at 281).

The courts seldom describe their reasoning in such cases, although one judge remarked that there was evidence that the accused had 'inclinations to serve others rather than to prey upon them' (*R.* v. *Ingham* at 185). Some have argued that this betrays a form of 'social accounting' on the part of the judiciary, whereby the offender's good points are allowed to balance his bad ones (Ashworth 1995b, p.142). It might be more accurate to say that the courts are allowing the defendant's good character to reduce his overdraft. Another suggestion is that judges see their role as one of moral reinforcement and choose their targets sparingly (Ashworth 1995b, p.142; Garland 1990, p.67). It is also possible, however, that in responding to these long-standing aspects of a defendant's character, the motivation of the courts is similar to that which operates when they consider those aspects of character which can be inferred from the crime. A defendant of good character is presumably less in need of being rehabilitated or of being deterred from doing the same thing again.

The other group of considerations relating to the offender concerns the likely effect of a sentence upon him. Bentham called this 'sensibility' (1823, p.72). The inconsistencies in this aspect of sentencing practice have already been mentioned.

The courts have generally been wary of allowing the unintended effects of punishment to influence their treatment of offenders (*R. v. Kay*). In some instances, exceptions have been made to allow the effect of imprisonment on the offender's career to be taken into account (*R. v. Stanley and Spindler* at 374, 375). This consideration is meant not to apply where the offence is intimately connected with the defendant's work (*R. v. Barrick* at 147) but Ashworth has argued that the courts may be more lenient than these Appeal Court cases suggest (Ashworth 1995b, p.143).[22]

The courts have also allowed the perceived vulnerability of the young (Thomas 1979b, p.195), old (*R. v. Wilkinson* [1974], unreported case quoted in Thomas 1979b, p.196) and pregnant women (*R. v. Beaumont*) to mitigate, as well as the likely effects of segregation upon the defendant (*R. v. Varden*) and any physical disability or illness which would subject him to an unusual degree of hardship in prison (*R. v. Herasymenko* [1975], quoted in Thomas 1979b, p.216). Finally, the Criminal Justice Act 1991 in England and Wales introduced a 'unit fines' system, whereby the offender's disposable income was allowed to influence the financial penalty for minor offences. The system proved controversial and was repealed by the Criminal Justice Act 1993. Nevertheless, under the new Act, courts must still take into account the offender's means when determining the amount of a fine (see Section 65[3] of the Criminal Justice Act 1993). Sensibility, at least economic sensibility, is thus allowed a role.

It is perhaps surprising that, if sensibility is allowed to influence sentencing at all, psychiatric considerations are not advanced more often. Those with phobias relating to confinement or contamination will be more distressed by a prison environment. The mentally handicapped may be subject to verbal and physical abuse, and the odd ideas and unusual behaviour of some people who suffer from schizophrenia may render them similarly vulnerable. And prison is no place to be sexually disinhibited, as are many sufferers from mania. It may be that judges are uncertain where consideration of psychiatric factors would end. Many people are peculiarly sensitive to experiences such as prison without suffering from psychiatric disorders. Should they not also receive special consideration? A criminal justice system which routinely allowed the sensibility of the defendant to influence sentencing might be functioning in a consistent manner, but it would be difficult to demonstrate that this was the case.

Many mentally disordered offenders are, however, dealt with by means of a psychiatric disposal after conviction (see p.46). Their crimes may be seen as different, perhaps partially excusable, by virtue of their state of mind when they acted. Sentencers may hope that the likelihood of reoffending will diminish if the offender receives treatment or may see the offence as providing an opportunity to act in the offender's best interests.[23] It is also likely, however, that judges and magistrates are reluctant to subject some mentally disordered defendants to the rigours of prison conditions.[24] That said, the most appropriate disposal for a defendant's mental health is only one consideration in sentencing. There are others, such as the protection of the public. Perhaps as a result, a substantial number of mentally disordered people are sent to prison (Gunn, Maden and Swinton 1991).

Other considerations

There are a number of other instances where the courts have shown a willingness to mitigate. One author has noted a tendency to treat more severely short-term visitors to this country (Walker 1985, p.47) and a custom of mitigating where there is an appearance of injustice in court proceedings (R. v. Ford). Where there is a substantial delay between the crime and the trial, the sentence is likely to be lighter than would otherwise be the case.[25]

PROVOCATION
Preliminary considerations

> Acts proceeding from anger are rightly judged not to be done of malice aforethought; for it is not the man who acts in anger but he who enraged him that starts the mischief. Again, the matter in dispute is not whether the thing happened or not, but its justice; for it is apparent injustice that occasions rage. (Aristotle, *Ethica Nicomachea*, 1135b)

The defence of provocation emerged in English law in the seventeenth century (Ashworth 1976). In order for someone who had killed to be found guilty of murder, the prosecution was required to show that he had acted with malice aforethought. If he had been provoked, he could avoid conviction by showing that this malice was absent (Hale 1736, p.455). In 1707 Lord Holt C.J. laid down five instances of provocation which included the striking of the accused, the sight of a friend or relative being beaten and the sight of a man in adultery with the wife of the accused.[26]

In England and Wales the Homicide Act 1957 made statutory provision for provocation to reduce what would otherwise be murder to manslaughter. The mandatory life sentence for murder can thus be avoided. The provocation may be by words or actions.[27] The jury is required to address two questions. First, was there a sudden and temporary loss of self-control? And second, would a reasonable person, in the circumstances of the defendant, have acted as he did? The first of these questions is usually referred to as the subjective test and the second as the objective test (Richardson 1999, ss.19.52–19.65; Smith and Hogan 1996, pp.361–377). For a defendant who has set up a defence of provocation to be convicted of murder, the prosecution must show that the answer to at least one of these questions is in the negative.

The subjective test: Loss of control

How is the jury to decide whether or not the defendant lost control? The appeal courts have provided little guidance. One nineteenth-century case made reference to the defendant being not the 'master of his own understanding' (R. v. Hayward at 159) and a recent case has repeated this wording (R. v. Ahluwalia at 138). Legal theorists refer to his 'snapping' or 'exploding' (Horder 1992, p.109). The defendant need not, however, have 'gone berserk' (R. v. Phillips at 137). The only qualification which the law makes is that the loss of control be 'sudden and temporary' (Lord Devlin in R. v. Duffy at 932).[28]

Can psychiatric factors affect what will be considered a loss of control? In R. v. Ahluwalia the defence argued that women who have been subjected to violent treatment over a long period suffer from 'battered woman syndrome'. They react differently from men to each act of provocation, demonstrating a 'slow-burn' as opposed to a sudden loss of self-control. When the Court of Appeal endorsed the judge's decision to leave to the jury the issue of whether provocation was present, some argued that the door had been opened to the defence of provocation becoming available to more 'battered women' (Nicolson and Sanghvi 1993). However, the Court of Appeal also endorsed Lord Devlin's requirement that the loss of control be 'sudden and temporary'. It is doubtful whether, as the law stands, the number of such defendants successfully pleading provocation will substantially increase (see Clarkson and Keating 1998, pp.693–706).[29]

The objective test

Before the Homicide Act 1957, provocation was part of the common law. The jury were required to ask themselves whether the behaviour of the victim would have led a reasonable or ordinary man to act as the defendant did (R. v. Welsh at 339). Two aspects of the reasonable or ordinary man were important. First, his level of self-control was normal. A defendant's defective self-control (R. v. Lesbini), even if it was the result of mental retardation (R. v. Alexander), was not relevant. Second, the reasonable man was assumed to be normal with regard to his general characteristics. Her pregnancy (R. v. Smith) or his impotence (R. v. Bedder), for instance, were not relevant, even if the provocation had been directed specifically at those characteristics.

The Homicide Act 1957 did not change the requirement that the defendant showed the self-control of the reasonable or ordinary man, although it has now been held that this means 'an ordinary person of the sex and age of the accused' (DPP v. Camplin at 718; see Ashworth 1995a, pp.269–273). The Act was, however, followed by the dropping of the requirement that the reasonable or ordinary man be normal in other respects. The jury are now required to clothe him in 'such of the accused's characteristics as they think would affect the gravity of the provocation' (DPP v. Camplin at 718). Some authors suggest that this change was the result of the Homicide Act placing more emphasis on the effects of verbal provocation than the common law had done (Smith and Hogan 1996, p.368). The likely effects of verbal provocation can only be assessed by taking into account some of the characteristics of the accused.

One might expect that this willingness on the part of the courts to clothe the reasonable man in the characteristics of the defendant would permit psychiatric factors to contribute to successful pleas of provocation. This has not happened. Legal theorists describe the partial defence as a concession to 'normal' human emotion and case law seems to bear this out (Ashworth 1976, pp.312 *et seq.*; Horder 1992, p.162). The courts have restricted the extent to which the reasonable man is to be clothed in the characteristics of the defendant, and done so in such a way that psychiatric factors are usually excluded. They have used two criteria.

First, the characteristic must be a permanent one, or, at least, sufficiently permanent to distinguish the offender from the ordinary person (Richardson 1999, s.19–62) and to be properly regarded as part of the defendant's 'character and personality' (*R. v. Newell* at 339). Transient states of mind, whether characterised by depression, excitability and irascibility, are not relevant. Second, there must be a 'real connection' between the nature of the provocation and the characteristic (*R. v. Newell* at 339). Thus, it would seem, if a mentally disordered defendant was taunted for having that disorder, then the disorder would be relevant. If the defendant was taunted about something else, however, the disorder will usually not be relevant to the issue of whether the reasonable man would have responded as the defendant did.[30]

One other criterion has recently been introduced and discarded. Alan Morhall was convicted of murder after stabbing a man who had repeatedly criticised him for his addiction to glue-sniffing. He appealed, arguing that he had been provoked. The Court of Appeal rejected his appeal, finding that, for the defendant to be found not guilty of murder, the characteristic in respect of which he had been provoked must not be discreditable. A further appeal to the House of Lords succeeded, however, when it was held that the credit which the characteristic did the defendant was not relevant to the issue of provocation (see *R. v. Morhall* and the commentary by Prof. Smith (1993)).

Criticism of the objective test

Some have argued that the requirement in the objective test – that the defendant should have done only what the reasonable or ordinary man would have done – is unfair to defendants whose personal characteristics lead them to lose control more easily than other people.[31] To the extent that acting under provocation is an excuse, so the argument goes, the courts should take into account all aspects of the mental state of the defendant.[32] The experiences of some people seem to lead them to lose control in particular situations. The psychiatric literature contains descriptions of veterans of the war in Vietnam who continued to react with disproportionate violence in situations which reminded them of combat (see Green, Wilson and Lindy 1985, pp.65–67; Keane *et al.* 1985, pp.258–259).

Ashworth, while acknowledging the problem, argues that in practice it does not lead to the conviction of defendants who should be excused (Ashworth 1976, pp.304–305). First, he contends, rational factors do affect what would usually be called 'emotional' behaviour, the likelihood of an aggressive response decreasing in proportion to the degree to which the provoker's actions are perceived as justified (Pastore 1952). Since these rational factors are common to all of us, Ashworth argues, our responses to a given level of provocation will be more uniform than would otherwise be the case. Second, individual differences in susceptibility to threats decrease as the intensity of the threat rises.[33] Ashworth is arguing that the answer to the question 'Did this defendant react in this way because he was provoked?' can usually be obtained by asking, 'Would the reasonable man have reacted in this way because he was provoked?'

This may not be the case. First, even if the likelihood of an aggressive response is reduced when the provoker's actions are perceived as justified, the level of any such response may show no such relationship with the degree of 'perceived justification'. Second, there are two reasons to doubt Ashworth's conclusion that differences in susceptibility to threats diminish as the level of threat rises. The authors to whom he refers measured physiological responses, such as muscle tension and pulse rates, to electronically generated 'white noise'. The stress and the nature of the subject's reaction to that stress are both very different from anything which would be invoked as part of a provocation defence. Additionally, their conclusion is that reactions to stress, far from being uniform, relate to 'personality traits…which produce a relatively stable proclivity to deal with stimuli in one way or another' (Oken *et al.* 1966, p.632).

In some cases, therefore, the conclusions which are reached using the 'reasonable-man' approach are probably different from those which would be reached if an attempt was made to take into account the individual's reaction to being provoked. Some evidence concerning individual reactions may be excluded, not because the 'reasonable-man' approach adequately takes these reactions into account, but because other defences are available for some defendants who react disproportionately.[34] A war veteran such as described above, charged with murder after reacting disproportionately to trivial provocation, might plead diminished responsibility if he could show that he suffered from an abnormality of mind.[35]

DIMINISHED RESPONSIBILITY

Preliminary considerations

The concept of diminished responsibility entered English law from Scotland, where the principle that 'weakness of mind' could reduce what would otherwise be regarded as murder to culpable homicide was first outlined in the 1870s by Lord Deas (*HM Advocate* v. *Dingwall*). The effect of Deas' judgement was to permit the courts to undertake what had previously been the prerogative of the monarch; namely, the substitution of a lesser sentence for one of death. In the view of Walker, this innovation was the result of the greater degree of judicial discretion available in Scotland at the time: the same development could not have happened in England where the definition of murder was more precise and where the criteria for insanity were more rigorous (Walker 1968, p.144). As Walker also points out, dissatisfaction with the rigidity of the English system was evident in the late nineteenth century. Fitzjames Stephen wrote that 'the law ought...where madness is proved, to allow the jury to return any one of three verdicts: Guilty; Guilty, but his power of self-control was diminished by insanity; Not Guilty on the ground of insanity' (1883, p.175).

It was to take until the middle of the twentieth century, however, before – on the advice of several of the witnesses who gave evidence to the Royal Commission on Capital Punishment (1953, pp.142–144) but against the majority recommendation of that Commission – the doctrine was introduced into English Law.

A successful plea of diminished responsibility leads to the defendant being found guilty not of murder but of manslaughter. The doctrine was introduced in England and Wales as Section Two of the Homicide Act 1957. This states:

> Where a person kills or is a party to the killing of another, he shall not be convicted of murder if he was suffering from such abnormality of mind (whether arising from a condition of arrested or retarded development of mind or any inherent causes or induced by disease or injury) as substantially impaired his mental responsibility for his acts or omissions in doing or being a party to the killing.

This wording was chosen despite the reservation voiced by Lord Denning, that the lack of criteria rendered the proposed doctrine too vague (Royal Commission on Capital Punishment 1953, Minutes Day 9, p.218), and despite the concern expressed by Dr Hopwood, Medical Superintendent of Broadmoor Institution, who gave evidence to the Commission that too much of the work of the court would be handed over to medical witnesses (Minutes Day 15, p.353).

About one-fifth of those who commit homicide are convicted of manslaughter after pleading not guilty to murder on the grounds of diminished responsibility (Dell 1984). The commonest diagnoses of those who make use of the plea are depression and schizophrenia, although sufferers from personality disorders, brain damage, epilepsy and the mentally impaired are also represented. The conclusions drawn by medical witnesses as to whether the criteria of Section Two were fulfilled were found by Dell to diverge in only 13 per cent of cases. In half of these the disagreement concerned the presence or absence of mental abnormality, and in the other half whether or not this abnormality was sufficient to reduce the defendant's responsibility. At the end of the 1970s, two-thirds of those who successfully pleaded diminished responsibility were sent to prison and one-third to hospital.

Lord Denning's reservations concerning the lack of criteria in the doctrine of diminished responsibility have been described. The wording of this part of the Homicide Act stems from that used to define 'mental defectives' in the Mental Deficiency Act 1927, and identifies a broad category ('abnormality of mind') which is then qualified by reference to its aetiology ('whether arising from a condition of arrested or retarded development of mind or any inherent causes or induced by disease or injury'). The defence has succeeded where the mental state of the accused would have had difficulty in meeting the criteria by which the M'Naghten Rules are usually applied (see Chapter 5). 'Despair' induced by the need to care for an imbecile child and a 'reactive depressed state' following the breaking of an engagement have both been held to amount to mental abnormality (Wootton 1960, p.229).

Mental function is commonly divided into the will and feelings, or volition, and the appreciation and manipulation of information, or cognition. Abnormalities of volition cannot usually contribute to a successful insanity defence (see p.88). The doctrine of diminished responsibility, however, does allow volitional factors a role. In R. v. Byrne (at 403), Lord Justice Parker held that 'abnormality of mind' referred to the ability not only to judge whether an act was right or wrong but also to exercise will-power to control one's actions.[36]

How are juries to decide whether an abnormality of volition is sufficient to reduce a defendant's responsibility? Appellate decisions usually place in opposition two elements: the impulse itself and the defendant's capacity for self-control.[37] In R. v. Byrne it was held that the difficulty which a defendant experienced in controlling his impulse should be substantially greater than that which would pertain for an ordinary man (see also the commentary on R. v. Simcox at 403). The impairment of control must be more than 'trivial' or 'minimal', but it need not be 'total' (R. v. Lloyd).

Criticism of the details

The wording of Section Two of the Homicide Act has been criticised on several grounds. First, it has been argued that 'abnormality of mind' is an extremely imprecise phrase, even when accompanied by its parenthetical qualification 'whether arising...'. The Butler Committee recommended that this section be changed so that a defendant would not be convicted of murder 'if there is medical or other evidence that he was suffering from a form of mental disorder as defined in Section 4 of the Mental Health Act 1959 and if, in the opinion of the jury, the mental disorder was such as to be an extenuating circumstance which ought to reduce the offence to manslaughter' (Committee on Mentally Abnormal Offenders 1975, p.247). The Mental Health Act 1959 defined 'mental disorder' as mental illness, arrested or incomplete development of mind, psychopathic disorder or 'any other disorder or disability of mind'. The Butler Committee's suggestion was endorsed by the Criminal Law Revision Committee of the Home Office (1980, p.39) and formed the basis of clause 38 of the codification proposals first published by the Law Commission in 1985. The proposals have not been enacted.

Griew has put forward a second criticism of the detail of the doctrine of diminished responsibility. He argues that the wording of Section Two, whereby mental abnormality is held substantially to diminish responsibility at law if it substantially impairs mental responsibility, is 'improperly elliptical' (Griew 1988, p.81). The wording is certainly problematic. The term 'responsibility' is used to refer both to a mental phenomenon ('impaired mental responsibility') and to a legal status ('diminished responsibility'). And an adjective with medical connotations ('impaired') is joined to a noun without medical meaning ('responsibility'). But the law's requirement, for a link between an abnormal mental condition and the act of killing, is less controversial. This requirement would be made more explicit, and Griew's improper ellipsis removed, if the wording were changed in line with Butler's suggestion or the Law Commission's criminal code, whereby a defendant would be not guilty of murder 'if, at the time of his act, he is suffering from such mental abnormality as is a substantial enough reason to reduce his offence to manslaughter' (Law Commission 1989, s.56[1]).[38]

A third criticism was touched on earlier. This is that no guidelines are provided to assist the jury. To quote the judges who gave evidence to the Butler Committee, 'if the jury think…that the defendant has shown recognisably abnormal mental symptoms and that in all the circumstances it would not be right to regard his act as murder in the ordinary sense, it is open to them to bring in a verdict of manslaughter' (Committee on Mentally Abnormal Offenders 1975, p.242). The wording of the section, and in particular the absence of criteria by which legal responsibility is to be assessed, has led to doctors testifying to what the American judge David Bazelon called the 'naked conclusion'[39] – namely, whether the accused can properly be held responsible for his actions. The view of a medical witness as to a defendant's responsibility for the act may be 'technically… inadmissible', but this has not stopped it being 'allowed time and time again without any objection' (Lord Parker in *DPP* v. *A. and BC Chewing Gum Ltd.* at 164).

In Bazelon's view this was inappropriate. Establishing the defendant's responsibility was the job of the jury.

There are two issues to be distinguished here. The first concerns the absence of criteria for the assessment of responsibility. This is not in itself sufficient to render the wording unsatisfactory. The potential for inconsistency in the decisions of different courts is certainly increased if no rules are available. But the suggestion that the task of assessing the criminal responsibility of mentally disordered offenders is best left to the jury with no statutory guidance has authoritative support (see Royal Commission on Capital Punishment 1953). The second issue concerns the frequency with which expert witnesses, in this case psychiatrists, are asked directly to address the question of responsibility. Does this make the wording unsatisfactory? That wording permits a doctor to describe the defendant's condition and its likely effect on him at the time he killed, leaving to the jury the task of deciding whether that condition amounted to an abnormality of mind and therefore reduced his responsibility.

It is likely that difficulties arise because the aspects of a defendant's mental state with which the jury is most concerned are those which pertain to the criminal act. The jury will wish to know, for instance, whether his feelings towards the victim had a pathological basis, and whether, at the time of the act, an abnormal mood state prevented him from controlling his actions. It is easy to see how, in answering these questions, psychiatrists are drawn into making statements which directly concern the defendant's responsibility for what he has done. This difficulty in drawing a line between the rightful provinces of jury and witness is not, however, a reason to change the wording of Section Two of the Homicide Act. It could be argued that it is an inevitable concomitant of a detailed assessment of criminal responsibility by the courts.

Criticism of the generality

Other critics of the doctrine of diminished responsibility hold that, legally, diminished responsibility is a contradiction in terms. To Sparks (1964), a defendant must be either responsible or not responsible for his actions. Someone who commits a criminal act 'either could, or could not, have avoided or refrained from committing it…there is no third possibility, midway between these two' (p.16). And, according to Sparks, if he could have refrained from committing it, there is no reason to reduce the severity of his punishment.

Sparks follows the choice theory of excuse (see p.34 above). He considers it unfair to blame or punish someone for something they have done unless they had both the ability and the opportunity to avoid doing it (p.9). He thinks that 'ability' and 'opportunity', in the sense in which he uses them, may be present to varying degrees. He refers, for instance, to 'partial' excuses (p.18) and points out that the capacity to conform to legal norms varies widely in both mentally normal and mentally abnormal populations (p.15). In Sparks' view, however, the critical question from the point of view of conviction is whether the defendant could have avoided committing the act in question. He recommends dispensing with the doctrine of diminished responsibility and adding a new clause to the insanity defence to allow the acquittal of a defendant who, 'owing to mental disorder or deficit, could not help committing the illegal act' (p.33).

I am not convinced. There are instances, apart from diminished responsibility, in which Anglo-American law recognises an intermediate point between complete and absent responsibility. The doctrine of provocation, described earlier, allows conviction for manslaughter instead of murder if certain criteria are fulfilled. One of these criteria is that the defendant should have lost control. That the law does not see this loss of control as an 'all-or-nothing' phenomenon is evident from Lord Diplock's reference to an 'intermediate stage' between icy detachment and going berserk (*Phillips* v. *R.* at 137) and from the doctrine's requirement that the 'out-of-control' defendant keep his response proportionate to the provocation.

Sparks could reply that the doctrine of provocation differs from diminished responsibility because it functions as a justification.[40] It is the wrongfulness of what the defendant has done which is regarded as less than would otherwise be the case, and the sentence is being mitigated in response to this diminished wrongfulness, not in response to diminished responsibility.[41] If provocation is not also a partial excuse, however, it is difficult to see why it should include any reference to loss of control.[42] The law's response to the partial excuse of provocation is to substitute a manslaughter conviction for one of murder. It seems inconsistent to recognise partial excuses for normal defendants but not for abnormal ones.[43]

The second point to be made in reply concerns the criteria which govern the provision of excuses in the criminal law. Sparks argues that the question to be answered before conviction is whether or not the defendant could have avoided acting as he did. No such wording exists in the defences available to normal defendants, however, such as duress and self-defence. Most defences available to the mentally abnormal similarly avoid any requirement that the defendant could have acted only as he did (see the discussion of the development of the insanity defence in Chapter 5). Only in the doctrine of 'irresistible impulse' is this implied, and this aspect of the doctrine has been heavily criticised (again, see Chapter 5). Indeed, unless the act was an involuntary one, it is difficult to see what evidence could be presented in court to show that a defendant could not have helped committing it. The issue is in many ways a philosophical one. Determinists would be easier to convince than advocates of free will.

In providing excuses to both normal and mentally abnormal defenders, the law concentrates instead on establishing whether the choice which the defendant made to act as he did was an adequate one. Factors which can render this choice inadequate include ignorance of the circumstances and coercion of various kinds. The M'Naghten Rules, for instance, exempt from punishment a sufferer from mental disease who was unaware either of the nature and quality of what he was doing, or that it was against the law. Awareness of what one is doing and knowledge of the law are not 'all or nothing'.

The M'Naghten Rules have been criticised for their emphasis on the defendant's levels of knowledge (see Chapter 5). As a result, certain legislatures in the United States have modified the insanity defence to include a reference to the defendant's capacity to control his actions. Sparks acknowledges that a lack of capacity to control one's actions is a proper basis on which to excuse, and that this capacity may be present to a greater or a lesser extent (Sparks 1964, p.10). It seems inconsistent to acknowledge this and simultaneously to demand that the law recognise only complete or absent responsibility.

Conclusion regarding diminished responsibility

Diminished responsibility, like provocation, exists to avoid the inflexibility of the mandatory life sentence for murder. It gives discretion to the sentencer where otherwise he would have none. The doctrine has been criticised both for the details of its wording in the Homicide Act 1957 and for the principles which would seem to underlie that wording. Three criticisms of the wording have been identified. These are that the phrase 'mental abnormality' is inexact, that the wording is circular (or, at least, 'elliptical') and that no criteria are provided to assist the jury in determining whether or not a defendant can properly make use of the defence.

It has been argued here that none of these criticisms give cause to abandon the doctrine. It has also been argued that, contrary to the views of some, it is appropriate to allow the reduced responsibility of some mentally abnormal defendants to be reflected in the sentences they receive. The arguments which have been put forward here do not relate to any particular offence or category of offences. As others have suggested, there seems no reason to continue to restrict the doctrine of diminished responsibility to murder.[44]

SUMMARY

One nineteenth-century author recommended exemplary sentences for those guilty of stealing such items as cattle and farm produce which, out of necessity, are stored in exposed positions. At the same time, he advocated leniency where the offender had been exposed to 'undue temptation' (Cox 1877, p.158). This tradition of inconsistency in the criteria employed to mitigate where no statutory guidance is offered has been maintained. In the second half of the twentieth century the criteria used by the courts have become more visible. This is due to the handing down of 'guideline' decisions by the Court of Appeal and the regular reporting of sentencing decisions. With regard to the statutory forms of mitigation, provocation and diminished responsibility, the criteria have been defined by statute and subsequent judicial development. Their visibility has been less of an issue, and debate has focused not on what criteria are being used, but on whether these criteria are correct.

With regard to the non-statutory forms of mitigation, there are three reasons why psychiatric factors might be taken into consideration by a judge or magistrate. First, such factors may offer the defendant a partial excuse because, owing to his condition, he was not able to choose to do as he did adequately. Second, sentencers may feel that the presence of a medical condition raises the possibility that treatment will reduce the chances of his reoffending. Finally, the judge or magistrate may feel that the psychiatrically disordered defendant would suffer unduly in prison. It is difficult to assess the degree to which these considerations affect sentencing. To the extent that they do so, they can result in the making of hospital orders or probation orders with psychiatric treatment as one of the conditions.

With regard to the doctrine of provocation, it has been argued here that the emphasis, in the criteria which require to be applied, on the behaviour of the 'reasonable man' makes it unlikely that psychiatric factors are admitted by the courts. Even when personal factors are allowed to operate, as when the defendant's characteristics are taken into account in deciding whether the provocation was sufficient to make him lose control, psychiatric factors have, at least until recently, not been discussed by the Court of Appeal. Psychiatric evidence is usually only admitted prior to conviction where the defendant is pleading a mental-state defence such as insanity. Mentally abnormal defendants charged with murder, however, will have their conviction reduced to one of manslaughter if they can show that their mental abnormality resulted in their responsibility being diminished.

NOTES

1. This wording is contained in: 'An Act to prevent the stealing of Linen, Fustian, and Cotton Goods and Wares, from Fields, Grounds and other Places used for whitening, bleaching or drying the same' (see 18 Geo. 2 c.27).

2. Bentham described the common law as 'judge-made law, stuffed...with tigers and jackalls, by whom, with the addition of a few land-crocodiles...the people are devoured' (Bentham 1843, p.575). For a detailed nineteenth-century codification proposal, see Beaumont (1821).

3. Authorities were divided as to whether or not this was a good thing. The Home Secretary described the variation in sentences passed down by different judges as 'one of the great scandals of our criminal jurisprudence' (Hansard, 2 April 1883, c.1227). At the same time, the discretion of the judge was regarded by reformers, at least when it led to leniency, as one of the 'most sacred principles' of English law (see Ruggles-Brise 1901, p.104).

4. See Thomas (1983). This tradition of inconsistency has survived the Criminal Justice Act 1991 (see Thomas 1993).

5. Those more sympathetic to retributive principles question the degree to which courts should do this (see Ashworth 1995b, p.146).

6. Hart (1968, p.15) distinguished 'formal' from 'informal' mitigation. 'Formal' mitigation, as provided by the doctrines of provocation and diminished responsibility, leads to conviction on a lesser charge.

7. Although mitigation is permitted in cases of provocation and diminished responsibility, it is not inevitable. A successful plea can still result in a life sentence.

8. There are, however, few Court of Appeal guidelines to this effect (see Walker 1985, p.47).

9. R. v. Ireland [1973]; R. v. Street and Gray [1974]; unreported cases quoted in Thomas 1979b, p.195.

10. R. v. Sang and Mangan at 263; although since this judgement, the grounds for mitigation in respect of entrapment have been steadily reduced (Thomas 1993).

11. R. v. Evans [1974], unreported case discussed by Thomas 1979b, p.372.

12. Explicit recognition of racially aggravated offences came with the Crime and Disorder Act 1998.

13. R. v. Evans [1974], unreported case discussed by Thomas 1979b, p.372.

14. The law formerly made a presumption that children under 14 could not be responsible for a criminal act. They were said to be 'doli incapax'. Section 34 of the Crime and Disorder Act 1998 removed this presumption, although it is still open to the child to prove that he lacks 'the mischievous discretion'.

15. It may also be, however, that he is seen as more amenable to rehabilitation.

16. In other words, judges are concerned here with general deterrence rather than individual deterrence.

17. When such evidence does affect sentencing, however, this may be the result, not of any perceived influence of the defendant's state on the circumstances of the offence, but of the courts' reluctance to send mentally disordered people to prison. The issue is also discussed on p.49.

18. R. v. Kirkland [1975], unreported case quoted by Thomas 1979b, p.172. These are Court of Appeal decisions. Magistrates' courts may be more willing to allow drunkenness as a mitigating factor. Intoxication is frequently put forward by the defence as grounds for mitigation (see Shapland 1981, p.56).

19. See the reference to 'the effect upon him, and indeed his wife, of loss of liberty' in R. v. Grant at 443.

20. In other words, when considering the defendant's character, judges have in mind individual deterrence. When taking into account the circumstances of the offence, it was argued on p.46, they have in mind general deterrence.

21. See R. v. Harper at 111: 'He is said to be a man who may respond to outside help.' See also Thomas 1979b, p.217.

22. Theft at work should be treated more severely because of the element of breach of trust which is present. The perpetrators of these crimes, however, are more likely than other thieves to have sabotaged their own careers. Research suggests that courts take this into account. In Moxon's study, sentence was suspended in 29 per cent of cases of theft in breach of trust but in only 15 per cent of other cases of theft (Moxon 1988, p.34).

23. A practice described by Walker and McCabe as 'occasionalism' (see Walker and McCabe 1973, p.101).

24. Some defendants might question whether the imposition of a hospital order was an example of the law being made 'more gentle'.

25. See R. v. Bird: the court remarked – 'The offence had not been changed by the passage of time, but the man had' (at 78).

26. See R. v. Mawgridge at 1115: 'For adultery is the highest invasion of property.'

27. The Homicide Act 1957, Section Three, refers to 'everything both done and said'.

28. Recent cases have confirmed that this still applies. See R. v. Ibrams and R. v. Thornton.

29. The list of conditions which can be invoked continues to be amended, however (see *R. v. Hobson*). The 1990s have seen suggestions that a new defence of self-preservation be introduced for women who kill their abusive male partners in the belief that they had no alternative (see Radford and Kelly 1995).

30. The law in this area has been subject to recent change and is not yet clear (see Clarkson and Keating 1998, pp.703–706; Richardson 1999, ss.19.60–19.62; Smith and Hogan 1996, p.371).

31. 'If the reason for excusing the "normal" man is that his innate control mechanism has been para- lysed by events, how can it be ethically proper to refuse the like benignity to a "sub-normal" man when his innate control mechanism has been so paralysed' (Turner 1964, p.535).

32. Two theories of excuse are described in Chapter 2. One, choice theory, holds that excuses exist when the actor did not make a proper choice to act as he did. The other, character theory, holds that excusable acts are acts which fail to reflect the actor's character. By either account, the law should consider the personal characteristics of a defendant before deciding whether or not he has an excuse.

33. Ashworth (1976) quotes the literature review conducted by Anthony (1972, p.6), who in turn quotes Oken *et al.* (1966).

34. The practice on the part of the courts of excluding psychiatric evidence prior to conviction unless one of the mental state defences is being run is described on p.32.

35. This is Ashworth's (1976) preferred solution. He would have more emphasis placed on the justifi- catory element of the doctrine of provocation, where in his view the emphasis historically lay. Those whose personal characteristics offer them an excuse should, he argues, be dealt with in other ways.

36. The dissenters on the Royal Commission on Capital Punishment (1953) were to suggest that a similar criterion be included in the insanity defence (see pp.109, 285–287 of the report).

37. Baroness Wootton described the beneficiaries of the defence as exhibiting 'diminished power to resist temptation, or, conversely, excessive sensibility to temptations not felt by others to be over- whelming' (Wootton 1960, p.231).

38. The Law Commission's proposal was based on a similar one by the Butler Committee. The Com- mittee preferred the term 'mental disorder' to 'mental abnormality'. The Law Commission's defi- nition of mental abnormality, however, is almost identical to that of mental disorder as it appears in the Mental Health Act 1983.

39. Bazelon 1974, p.21; the judge was referring to the Durham Rule in the USA.

40. Although he would have to argue that it was only a partial justification. If provocation was a com- plete justification, it should presumably result in an acquittal. The concept of a partial justification is not widely discussed. The term is used, however, by Ashworth (1976, p.307) and Horder (1992, p.85).

41. He would obtain some support from Ashworth (1976) for this view. But Ashworth thinks that provocation functions simultaneously as an excuse.

42. And the loss of control limb is essential to the defence: 'If D is of an unusually phlegmatic temper- ament and it appears that he did not lose his self-control, the fact that a reasonable man in like cir- cumstances would have done so will not avail D in the least' (Smith and Hogan 1996, p.364).

43. Especially if, like Sparks, one believes that 'to assert that a man is mentally abnormal...is not to as- sert, or even normally to imply, anything whatever about his...liability to blame or legal punishment' (Sparks 1964, p.11).

44. See Mackay 1995, p.206. Walker (1993) refers to this restriction as a 'historical accident' (p.208).

CHAPTER 4

How Can Mental States Excuse?

We justify largely on the basis of factors outside the mind of the actor, but we excuse on the basis of internal factors, usually relating to that actor's motivation for doing as he or she did: whether he or she truly had a choice and, perhaps, whether we are able to infer a 'bad' character from a particular act. In considering choice, we want to know whether the actor had, first, the capacity and, second, the opportunity to have acted differently. The purpose of this chapter is to examine the mechanisms by which psychiatric factors affect capacity, opportunity and the soundness of inferences regarding the actor's character.

The meaning of capacity and opportunity were discussed in Chapter 2. Hart used the term 'opportunity' to refer to the external circumstances which constrain the actor. 'Capacity' he employed to refer to an actor's own abilities. These abilities he divided in turn into the intellectual and the volitional.[1] Not all authors agree with Hart's demarcation. Lacey places volition within the ambit of opportunity: '...a person must both understand the nature of her actions, knowing the relevant circumstances and being aware of the possible conse-quences, and have a genuine opportunity to do otherwise than she does – to exercise control over her actions, by means of choice' (1988, p.63). Whether part of capacity or part of opportunity, the mental faculties involved in choice are being divided according to whether they relate to the intellect or to the will. This analysis echoes the grounds for removal of blame put forward by Aristotle in *Ethica Nicomachea* (at III, 1); namely, that the actor did as he did out of ignorance or under compulsion.

Lacey's concepts correspond closely to the categories currently employed to classify mental phenomena. Instead of understanding, knowledge and awareness, however, psychiatrists and psychologists more often refer to consciousness, thinking, believing, perceiving and attending. Instead of control, they talk in terms of emotion (or affect) and impulsivity. The first part of this chapter will review the effects of psychiatric conditions on these mental phenomena. An effect, however, does not amount to an excuse. The second part of the chapter will discuss the difficulties which attend establishing whether or not the presence of a psychiatric condition can be grounds for exculpation.

THE EFFECTS OF PSYCHIATRIC CONDITIONS ON MENTAL PROCESSES

Consciousness

Consciousness[2] has been described as a continuum between full alertness and coma. People with reduced levels, or 'clouding', of consciousness frequently appear drowsy, although small deviations from full alertness result only in subtle impairments of thinking, attending, perceiving and remembering (Lishman 1978, p.5). Reduced consciousness is characteristic of the so-called 'acute organic reactions', conditions with an abrupt onset caused by various pathological processes affecting the brain. These include space-occupying lesions such as tumours and blood clots, infections such as meningitis and encephalitis and metabolic disorders such as liver disease and porphyria. The latter condition, widely believed to have affected George III (see Macalpine and Hunter 1969), is of genetic origin and usually surfaces in the third or fourth decades of life. In addition to clouding of consciousness, it is associated with mood changes and, occasionally, violent behaviour.

A number of conditions can cause complex and, less commonly, purposive acts of which the actor is unaware. Some medical writers use the term 'automatism' to describe all such acts, but most use it to refer only to automatic behaviour associated with epilepsy (see Fenwick 1990; Lishman 1978, pp.370–374). Confusingly, the term 'automatism' also has a legal meaning which will be discussed in Chapter 5. Automatic behaviour in epilepsy is more likely when the focus lies in the medial part of the temporal lobe. It is usually of brief duration but may last for up to an hour (Lishman 1978, pp.317–319). Criminal behaviour is rare (Gunn and Fenton 1971). Complex, apparently purposive acts occurring in reduced consciousness are also associated with hypoglycaemia, alcohol intoxication and sleep-walking (Fenwick 1990).

Cutting (1985, pp.223–224) has described three symptoms of schizophrenia which affect the level of consciousness.[3] These are perplexity, depersonalisation and oneirophrenia. Perplexity has been described, for medical purposes, as, 'the oppressive awareness of one's inability to cope with a given internal or external situation, this awareness being experienced as something which cannot be explained, something that has to do with one's own self' (Storring 1939, p.79). It is characterised by statements such as, 'I don't know what is going on', apparent disorientation on initial questioning (but often no such disorientation on further testing), and a puzzled facial appearance and bewilderment (Hoch and Kirby 1919). It may accompany the acute stage of schizophrenia (Hamilton 1985, p.76) and some authors have described it as characteristic of cycloid psychosis.[4]

Depersonalisation has been defined as a state in which 'the individual feels completely changed from what he was previously. The change is present in the ego as well as in the outside world and the individual does not recognise himself as a personality. His actions appear to him as automatic. He observes his actions and behaviour from the point of view of a spectator' (Schilder 1935, p.138).[5] Opinions vary as to whether it is typical of schizophrenia. Langfeldt (1960) regarded it as a critical diagnostic feature, but used a much broader definition of depersonalisation than Schilder. Other authors have reported it in only a minority of cases (see Mayer-Gross 1935).[6] Oneirophrenia is a condition present in some cases of schizophrenia in which the subject's experience is said to be pervaded by a dream-like quality.[7] The term was employed widely in the first half of the twentieth century but its use has since become less common. The most recent edition of the *International Classification of Diseases* (ICD) subsumes oneirophrenia under 'acute schizophrenia-like psychotic disorder' (World Health Organisation 1992, p.103).

Dissociative states are characterised by an alteration in consciousness of relatively sudden onset (Kendell and Zealley 1993, p.513). They are seen principally in neurosis, but may also be present in psychosis and in normal people under stress (see Cutting 1985, p.223). They have been described as conditions in which the subject allows or denies entry into consciousness to events or aspects of the environment which are not usually amenable to such manipulation (Cutting 1985, p.222). Thus the main feature of dissociative amnesia is a loss of memory, usually of important or stressful recent events, which is not due to brain damage or fatigue. Dissociative fugues also involve a loss of memory but also an apparently purposeful journey, usually away from home, during which the subject continues to look after himself to his normal standard. Modern systems of classification (World Health Organisation 1992, pp.151–161) include, in the dissociative disorders, trances and possession states, convulsions and instances of paralysis where no physical explanation can be found and which, in previous classifications, would probably have been called hysterical.

Also included under the dissociative states in modern classifications are the so-called multiple personality disorder and Ganser's syndrome. The latter was first described in criminals awaiting trial for serious crimes and is characterised by the subject's answering a question incorrectly in such a way that he seems to be doing so deliberately. Kendell and Zealley provide as an example the case of a man who when asked how many legs a horse had, replied 'five' (1993, p.515). In the example provided by Hamilton, a patient asked to say when the First World War started gave the date of her birth; when she was then asked for her date of birth she answered 1914 (1985, pp.57–58). Multiple personality is characterised by the adoption of one or more new and different personalities into which the individual switches from time to time. Each of these personalities is markedly different from the subject's own and appears to have no knowledge of its rivals.[8]

The dissociative states are supposed to be defences against anxiety. As Hamilton has pointed out, since almost every symptom of mental disorder has been described as a defence against anxiety, this can hardly be regarded as a distinguishing feature (Hamilton 1985, p.75). Nevertheless, in this instance the descriptions make a convincing case for the involvement of stress in the aetiology. David Livingstone, relating his experience of being seized by a lion, described 'a sense of dreaminess in which there was no sense of pain nor feeling of terror, though I was quite conscious of all that was happening' (Hamilton 1985, p.75). Forensic psychiatrists report cases of dissociative fugue in subjects who have just committed a criminal act as well as in some who face imminent detection (Gunn and Taylor 1993, p.430).

For the purposes of the criminal law, however, the difficulty is that defences against anxiety need not be unconscious. The example of hysterical fugue (what would now be called dissociative fugue) used in many of the older psychiatric texts was originally provided by William James (1891).[9] It concerns the Reverend Ansel Bourne who disappeared from his home in Providence, Rhode Island, and came to himself two months later working as a shopkeeper in a town 200 miles away. Bourne had withdrawn a large sum of money from his bank immediately before leaving Providence. The obvious conclusion is that the loss of memory and the new personality were both part of his efforts to escape for a few months from some local difficulty. Hamilton's suggestion is that a pregnant Sunday school teacher had miscarried by the time he recovered (Hamilton 1985, p.64). Similar reservations have been expressed with regard to other dissociative phenomena. Some experienced psychiatrists remain unconvinced that they have ever seen a case of dissociative amnesia (as opposed to lying) (Hamilton 1985, p.64) and failure to remember has been described as the most frequently feigned mental disorder (Anderson 1964, p.264). Malingering is one suggested explanation for Ganser's syndrome (Lishman 1978, p.564).

The cause of multiple personality was set back considerably by the case of Kenneth Bianchi, the Californian 'Hillside Strangler', who faked multiple personality and hypnosis in order to avoid the death penalty (Kendell and Zealley 1993, p.515), and the *International Classification of Diseases* (ICD) remarks that it is unclear to what extent the syndrome is the product of medical interest (World Health Organisation 1992, p.160).[10] The case for a wider recognition of the possible excusing effect at law of multiple personality has been made by referring to the inability of the 'primary', law-abiding, personality to 'know' what the 'secondary', lawbreaking, personality was doing. By this argument the defences of insanity and diminished capacity both become available[11] and there are reports of multiple personality successfully forming the basis of an insanity defence.[12]

Not all psychiatrists are sympathetic to such developments. In the United States, some authors have referred to multiple personality being 'spuriously' reported (Ludolph 1985, p.1527). Forensic psychiatrists in Britain have been frankly sceptical of the ability of one personality to exist in ignorance and under the sway of another personality in the same body.[13] Halleck (1990) has offered several reasons to doubt the contention of someone suffering from multiple personality disorder that 'someone else did it'. The fact that treatment is often sought to 'fuse' the multiple personalities suggests that the subject has at least a latent ability to control dissociation. The reported success of such treatment offers further support to this view. Some sufferers are able to switch from one personality to another at will, and many people with multiple personality knowingly mislead others about their condition.[14]

Nevertheless, the capacity for people in dissociative states to act in ways which are out of character is well recognised. Even those who question whether this can rightfully be described as evidence of multiple personality acknowledge that dissociative behaviour can include criminal acts.[15] If, as modern definitions make clear, dissociative states result in 'a partial or complete loss of the normal integration between memories of the past, awareness of identity and immediate sensations and control of bodily movements' (World Health Organisation 1992, p.151), it would seem inevitable that the subject's capacity and opportunity to act otherwise than he did have been reduced. The point at issue might best be said to be the degree to which this is the case. One author has suggested that, while those who are described as demonstrating multiple personalities should not be exempted from punishment, our moral and legal response should recognise that they are other than 'normal' and 'mature' individuals (see Gillet 1986, p.184). Some contend that for these reasons evidence of multiple personality should be allowed to go to mitigation (see Gunn and Taylor 1993, p.430).[16]

Emotion

One might expect the effect of psychiatric conditions upon the emotions to be of particular relevance to responsibility. Modern writing on the philosophy of action holds that action is driven by a combination of desire and belief. Desire is described in similar terms to those psychiatrists use when they refer to affect.[17] Eugene Bleuler, the professor of psychiatry in Zurich who first suggested the term 'schizophrenia', emphasised the role of affect in the genesis of action: 'Action is for the most part influenced by affectivity, if one at least agrees with us when we designate the force and direction of the impulses, or of the "will" as partial manifestations of the affects. He who is happy, sad or furious will react accordingly' (1924, p.143). He received contemporaneous support from Bernard Glueck in the United States:

> The motives for all indulgence or abstinence in behaviour are derived from emotional tones (pleasurable or unpleasurable imagery, attraction and repulsion, strivings and counter-strivings). Upon the strength of these feelings depends the intensity of the motive, and by the same token, the urge for action. In the battle of

motives, the decision rests with the side which possesses the preponderance of affectivity. (Glueck 1919, p.158)

Which psychiatric conditions are likely to influence this preponderance?

The obvious candidates are the so-called affective disorders, depression and mania. The terminology in this area can be confusing. People may suffer from repeated episodes of depression without ever becoming manic. Those who have only ever been manic, however, are very likely to experience an episode of depression at some point and are therefore said to suffer, along with those who have experienced episodes of both, from 'manic-depression'.[18] Mania and depression are characterised by a pervasive change in behaviour. In depression this usually consists of a general slowing and reduction in the quantity of movement although some people become agitated and may do more, albeit in a less-than-useful way. In mania the reverse occurs. Sufferers are overactive to an extent that may lead to physical exhaustion. They embark upon numerous new activities, which they frequently fail to finish.

But the overall level of activity is not of great importance for the purposes of excusing on psychiatric grounds. Depressed people may do less, but this is unlikely to constitute a crime. There are exceptions: a pilot might fail to check his fuel or a lorry driver omit to secure his load.[19] The pilot and the lorry driver would be doing less in all areas of their lives, however, not just those areas which impinged on the safety of others. In some respects the breach of the law is an unfortunate consequence of their choice of employment. Criminal charges stemming from such 'crimes of omission' are likely to be uncommon. Similarly, the fact that manic people do more does not lead to an overall increase in violent behaviour (see Craig 1982; Hafner and Boker 1973, pp.299–300; Krakowski, Volavka and Brizer 1986; Schipkowensky 1968). When an abnormal mood state is linked to a belief, however, behaviour can be directed at achieving a goal.

Thus eye surgeons treat self-induced ocular injuries in people who are depressed and who describe delusions of guilt (see Albert, Burns and Scheie 1965). People who suffer from mania may act to harm themselves in the presence of similar abnormal beliefs (see Hartmann 1925).[21] And in depression the frequency of suicide attempts has been found to be related to the presence of delusions (Miller and Chabrier 1988). Some criminal acts by depressed people also occur in the context of delusions,[22] a point emphasised by West (1965, pp.105–106). Thus one of his sample gassed herself and her child, believing incorrectly that she was pregnant and that she would be unable to survive another birth; another expressed a groundless fear of cancer before committing murder.

The cases cited by West illustrate two points about the role of mood states in the genesis of criminal acts. First, they serve to alter the background against which decisions are taken. The woman who chose to gas herself rather than go through another birth explained in her suicide note her reason for killing the child as well as herself: she did not want her husband to have to endure the difficulties of bringing their child up on his own. As a reason for killing someone, this seems quite inadequate, and there is no suggestion in West's account that this was her normal form of reasoning. It is more likely that many of the premises on which she was basing her decisions had been altered by her illness. The quality of life which the child could expect would be poor. The chances of its dying anyway from neglect or disease would be high. Her husband, frustrated by his inability to cope with childcare, might be violent towards the baby. And so on. Through such distortions[23] the 'right' thing to do becomes a very different thing from what it was before.[24]

Second, it is clear that mood changes and beliefs are insufficient to explain many criminal acts. Crimes of violence are not the usual consequence of the coincidence of mood changes and delusions. West tried to identify risk factors for violent acts in depressives and concluded that personality factors and the length of the subject's illness were more important (West 1965, pp.105–106). In particular, he believed that violent acts were more likely as the subject started to recover and became more active. With regard to mania, it has been suggested that subjects with a persecutory flavour to their symptomatology (Biegel and Murphy 1971) and those in the middle of an episode of illness (Carlson and Goodwin 1973) are more likely to commit crimes, although others have questioned whether it is possible to distinguish such categories (Wulach 1983).[25]

Psychiatric disorders other than depression and mania may also affect the emotions. European psychiatrists in the first half of the twentieth century believed that a pervasive emotional deficit was one of the characteristic features of schizophrenia. To Kraepelin there was 'a weakening of those emotional activities which permanently form the mainsprings of volition' (1913, p.74), while to Bleuler (1911) a disturbance of affectivity was one of the four cardinal signs of the condition. Recent reviewers agree. Cutting's (1985) conclusion is that the characteristic disorder in schizophrenia is a reduction in the capacity to experience and communicate emotion (p.238). There is experimental evidence to this effect. In one study, people with schizophrenia and controls were shown pictures in pairs and asked to say whether the theme of each pair was consistent. The subjects with schizophrenia did worse than controls when the theme was an emotional one such as affection or reprimand, but performed normally when the theme related to a geometric composition (Turbiner 1961). In another experiment, people with chronic schizophrenia were compared with controls with regard to their ability to recognise the emotions present in photographs of faces. The people with schizophrenia were correct 44 per cent of the time against the controls' 78 per cent (Dougherty, Bartlett and Izard 1974).

Paradoxically, there is also evidence that in many respects people with schizophrenia are more sensitive than others to emotional issues. Thus the disorder in the form of speech, a common feature of the disease, becomes more pronounced when the sufferer is describing emotive, rather than neutral, pictures (Feldstein 1962). And a large body of research shows that people with schizophrenia are more likely to relapse if their home environment is emotionally fraught (Vaughn and Leff 1976). In addition, while the most common and pervasive disturbance of mood is 'blunting' or 'flattening' of affect, the textbooks also make reference to 'incongruity', as when the sufferer laughs at news of a bereavement (see Gelder, Gath and Mayou, 1983 p.230). It has been suggested that flattening of affect allows people with schizophrenia to injure themselves as a consequence of their delusions (Shore 1979): the effect of the illness is presumably to insulate the sufferer from the emotive aspects of what they are doing. Others have argued that blunting is associated with violence to others (Mullen 1988).

Impulsiveness

What of people who, in the words of the German philosopher and psychologist Hoffbauer (1808, p.17, quoted in Barras and Bernheim 1990), are 'for the main part entirely reasonable persons, with sound judgement in all matters and without a trace of erroneous sentiment, yet are impelled by an irresistible force to commit certain actions'? The idea that people can be forced by impulses beyond their control to engage in acts which they would not otherwise engage in has been received sceptically by both courts and doctors. An Australian judge described the suggestion that the Almighty had created beings whom He exposed to temptation without giving them the power to resist as 'a direct impeachment upon the wisdom and goodness of Providence' (LEGE 1844, p.309). A forensic psychiatrist, reviewing the issue recently, finds it difficult to see how the concept has survived for so long (Mawson 1990). Yet some people do seem to lack a normal ability to control their behaviour.

Shore (1979) described the case of a patient, found with a pencil lodged in his right eye, who quoted Matthew 5:29: 'And if thy right eye offend thee, pluck it out, and cast it from thee, for it is profitable for thee that one of thy members should perish, and not that thy whole body should be cast into Hell.' The literature also describes the case of a man who mutilated his genitals invoking a similar passage at Matthew 18:7–9 (Greilsheimer and Groves 1979). Waugh's patient castrated himself in response to a later passage at Matthew 19:12: 'There are eunuchs born that way from their mother's womb, there are eunuchs made so by men and there are eunuchs who have made themselves that way for the sake of the Kingdom of Heaven' (Waugh 1986). Maudsley described the case of a 72–year-old woman whose illness led her to make repeated and unprovoked attacks on her daughter to whom, between episodes, she was very attached (Maudsley 1897, p.156).

Perhaps even closer to Hoffbauer's idea of impulsion is the phenomenology of obsessive compulsive disorder (OCD). This is described in the *International Classification of Diseases* (ICD) as a state where, 'the outstanding symptom is a feeling of subjective compulsion – which must be resisted…to carry out some action, to dwell on an idea…the obsessional urge or idea is recognised as alien to the personality but as coming from within the self. Obsessional actions may be quasi-ritual performances designed to relieve anxiety' (World Health Organisation 1978, p.36; see also World Health Organisation 1992, pp.142–143). There are two potential sources of action resulting from obsessional impulses.

The first is that the sufferer fails to resist his impulse. In OCD these impulses frequently relate to violent or sexually inappropriate acts, and might therefore be expected to be of relevance to the criminal law. Acting in this way as a result of obsessional thoughts is extremely rare, however, and may be modified by the subject. Marks cites the case of a woman who experienced impulses to kill her two-year-old child but sacrificed a pet tortoise instead (Marks 1987, p.431). This ability to alter the behaviour which one exhibits in response to obsessional thoughts would presumably reduce the excusing effect of such thoughts. The second possibility is that the ritualistic behaviour – in which the subject indulges in an attempt to alleviate the anxiety associated with obsessional thoughts and impulses – itself constitutes a criminal act. Most behaviour consists of washing or checking rituals, however, and although activities such as looking after children can be compromised, the law is seldom broken.

The controversy which has surrounded the notion of irresistible impulse, and which will be returned to in the next chapter, may in part have stemmed from a misunderstanding of the different ways in which psychiatric phenomena can contribute to impulsive behaviour. The impulses of OCD are experienced as alien and often as absurd. Any associated behaviour is usually, in terms of the criminal law, trivial. Delusions, on the other hand, are fixed beliefs which are often defended by the subject. Especially where the subject's mood is affected (see p.68), they can be associated with violence. In such instances, however, it is a moot point whether there is an impulse and, if there is, whether it can truly be said to be 'irresistible'. It might be better to say that the psychological mechanisms by which we regulate our behaviour have been distorted, either by mood changes or by other aspects of the illness.[26]

Perception

The effect on perception of the affective psychoses has already been mentioned. The bleak colouring of the perceptions of depressed people are widely recognised and can lead to violent acts when they contribute to a belief that one's own, or someone else's, life is pointless. The perceptual changes in schizophrenia are more complex. Older writers suggested that perception was normal (Bleuler 1911, p.56; Kraepelin 1913, p.5); more recent reviewers have demurred (see Cutting 1985, pp.285 *et seq.*). The argument would seem to hinge on the point at which perception can be said to end and thinking to begin. Basic perception, as measured, for instance, by the length of exposure required for something to be recognised, is normal (Magaro and Page 1982). What seems to be lacking is some aspect of the ability to deal with the information received. Thus people with schizophrenia are less able to identify happiness, sadness, joy and anger from photographs (Muzekari and Bates 1977). While this may in part be the result of their difficulty in experiencing emotion, it has been suggested that such failure is also due to a tendency to concentrate on the details of what is presented rather than the whole (Reich and Cutting 1982). Arieti's (1966) term for this was 'awholism'.

The specificity of the change in emotional responsiveness which can occur as a consequence of disease is even more dramatic in relation to head injury. In one case a man was able to react emotionally to his perceptions only when these were visual (see Bauer 1982). All scenery seemed the same, so he gave up hiking; all women looked uninspiring, so he gave up *Playboy.* He continued to derive a normal emotional reaction from listening to music or from touching delicate fabrics. This description is unusual. The literature on head injuries contains many examples of agnosias – failures of recognition not due to defective sensory apparatus. Such failures may be sense-specific: in prosopagnosia a patient may be unable to recognise a relative or friend from their appearance, but can do so once the person starts to speak (see Frederiks 1969, p.17). People may even fail to recognise their own faces in the mirror (see De Ajuriaguerra, Strejilevitch and Tissot 1963). The agnosias, however, are not usually described as affecting the subject's emotional response to the object which he or she is attempting to recognise. The propensity of schizophrenia to produce such an effect may be more likely to lead to changes in behaviour.

The most striking examples of altered perception, however, are hallucinations. These are succinctly defined as perceptions without objects[27] and can occur in any of the sensory modalities. Thus people describe hearing voices when there is nobody nearby, smells and tastes for no apparent reason and seeing things which are not there. Hallucinations are associated with numerous conditions including depression (when auditory hallucinations are frequently derogatory or accusatory), schizophrenia, epilepsy (when they may consist in unusual odours) and toxic confusional states (as when a severe infection is associated with visual hallucinations).

Thinking and believing

Some conditions which interfere with thinking affect previously healthy individuals; others are present from the early years of life. The most obvious examples of the latter are the various forms of mental retardation, characterised by low performance on all kinds of intellectual tasks including learning, remembering, using concepts and solving problems. It is customary in the United Kingdom to subdivide the condition according to the level of intelligence on formal testing: 'profound' mental retardation thus refers to an IQ of less than 20; 'severe' 20–34; 'moderate' 35–49; and 'mild' 50–70. It is unsatisfactory to hold strictly to these numerical categories, however, and most authors emphasise the importance of assessing social functioning when making the diagnosis (see Gelder *et al.* 1983, p.687). In addition, IQ is usually broken down into its various sub-tests for the purposes of accurate description and therapeutic intervention. These sub-tests examine such areas as vocabulary, the capacity to arrange pictures in a logical sequence and the ability to identify similarities in a series of geometrical designs.

Other conditions which are present from childhood exert a less general effect. Prominent among these is infantile autism, also called Kanner's syndrome after the psychiatrist who first described it (see Kanner 1943). The characteristic features are the so-called 'autistic aloneness', whereby the child is unable to make warm emotional relationships with people; a speech and language disorder (although about half of people with autism acquire some useful speech); and a tendency to become distressed when routines change.[28] Autistic children vary greatly in their intellectual performance – IQ scores range from 'severe' retardation to well above the average for the general population – but about three-quarters show some degree of impairment. This appears to be related to the ability to process information, and in particular information relating to emotion (see Rutter and Hersov 1985, pp.550–551). Attempts to describe the deficit in more specific terms have generally been unfruitful. Autistic children seem to have difficulty in predicting how others will act in a given situation (see Baron-Cohen, Leslie and Frith 1985). It has also been suggested that they have an inability to empathise (see Rutter and Schopler 1987 for a review).

Of particular interest in the context of the criminal law is the syndrome of 'autistic psychopathy', also known eponymously as Asperger's syndrome.[29] Sufferers are unable to share feelings fully, as when a friend's bad news makes us sad. Their speech and areas of interest betray a pedantic and literal approach to reasoning. Children with Asperger's syndrome generally speak better than those with autism, and their social behaviour, although one-sided and awkward, does not display the aloofness evident in Kanner's syndrome (see Wing 1981). Nevertheless, Asperger's syndrome and infantile autism may be variants of the same condition.[30] It has been suggested that children with Asperger's syndrome are especially prone to violent behaviour, the implication in such descriptions being that their inability to empathise with their victims allows them to indulge in acts which would otherwise be psychologically impossible (Gunn and Taylor 1993, pp.395–396). Similar suggestions have been made with reference to the violent behaviour of some adult sufferers (Mawson, Grounds and Tantum 1985). Unfortunately, the psychological functioning of sufferers from Asperger's syndrome has been studied much less than is the case for autism and the nature of the psychological deficit is even less clear.

Some would not hesitate to ascribe a similar causation – namely, a biologically determined inability to empathise – to the callousness of many of those labelled as suffering from 'antisocial personality disorder'.[31] In 1786 Benjamin Rush coined the term 'anomia' for a lack of conscience in certain of his patients (see Carlson and Simpson 1965). A century later, on the other side of the Atlantic, Maudsley stated: 'As there are persons who cannot distinguish certain colours, having what is called colour blindness, and others who, having no ear for music, cannot distinguish one tune from another, so there are some who are congenitally deprived of moral sense' (Maudsley 1897, p.62). A similar analysis would seem to underlie Cleckley's account of psychopathy with his references to 'obviously pathologic' behaviour and the 'central disorder' of the psychopath (Cleckley 1964, pp.43, 268). The difficulties with such assertions are several. First, the reliability of the diagnosis is low (see Gunn and Robertson 1976; Walton and Presly 1973). For this reason, it is difficult to know whether different authors are talking about the same group of symptoms and signs.

Second, such abnormalities as have been found are present only in sub-groups of people with antisocial personalities. Thus one study of men convicted of violent offences divided the sample into those who were habitually aggressive and those who had demonstrated only a single outburst of violence. Fifty-seven per cent of the habitually aggressive group had abnormal brainwaves, as detected by electroencephalogram (EEG), as against 12 per cent of the single outburst group (Williams 1969). Finally, the research findings are inconsistent: in the study just mentioned, the most common site of EEG abnormalities was the anterior temporal region. Earlier work had suggested that antisocial people showed an excess of slow waves in the posterior temporal region (Hill 1952). It is not clear whether these issues will eventually be clarified. Aubrey Lewis, acknowledging the 'wavering confines' of the category, at least thought that there was a category there to be defined.[32] Others have argued that the concept of antisocial personality is fatally flawed.[33]

Other psychiatric conditions which affect thinking and believing arise later in life. The reduced ability of those with dementia to identify people and the likely consequences of actions is well known. Perhaps the most obvious example, however, of illness affecting thinking and believing is delusions.

The definition of delusion has engaged psychiatrists and others in debate for many years (Hamilton 1985, pp.43–53). In essence, delusions are beliefs which are firmly held despite evidence to the contrary, not including conventional beliefs, such as religious convictions, which the person might be expected to hold given their educational and cultural background.[34] Thus a sufferer from the Capgras syndrome believes that someone – frequently closely involved with the sufferer and often a family member – is not who they claim to be and is in fact a double. Weinstock (1976) described the case of a young man who attacked his parents with a meat cleaver, seriously injuring his mother. He was convinced that the people he had attacked were machine-like beings who had stolen him from his real parents. Another sufferer made elaborate plans to torture his parents and children, believing that they were strangers who were being paid to spy on him by a foreign power (Crane 1976). Delusions can also alter the way in which the consequences of acts are seen. Jones describes the case of a man with schizophrenia who touched his ear repeatedly, explaining that this controlled the pumping of his blood (Jones 1965).

Attention

Attention has been divided into four components (see Cutting 1985, p.207). First, there is the capacity in the resting state to monitor what is happening; this capacity is termed 'vigilance'. Second, once one has been vigilant enough to notice that something is going on, there is the ability to follow this for a period of time; this is called 'attention span'. Third, there is the ability to select the object of one's attention from the mass of other things which may be going on simultaneously (Posner and Boies 1971). Finally, there is the ability to stop paying attention to one thing and move on to another (Zubin 1975). All of these elements of attention are profoundly affected by depression. Cutting (1985) found that 80 per cent of his sample of depressed subjects admitted to poor attention as a symptom (p.181), and the psychiatric texts generally make reference to the related phenomenon of lack of concentration when reviewing depressive symptomatology (Gelder et al. 1983, p.189).

Attention is also affected in schizophrenia (Freedman 1974; Freedman and Chapman 1973; McGhie and Chapman 1961). Vigilance is usually measured by a 'continuous performance test', where subjects sit in front of a revolving drum on which are written the letters of the alphabet. They are then given a letter to look out for and press a button when this letter appears. Normal subjects miss two letters out of 50 (Kornetsky and Orzack 1978); in one study, 45 per cent of testable subjects with schizophrenia missed three or more (Garmezy 1978). The effect of schizophrenia upon attention span is more controversial. The subject's capacity can be measured in two ways. First, they may be presented with information aurally, usually a sequence of digits, and asked to repeat as much of the sequence as possible. Normal subjects are expected to manage seven digits when repeating them in the same order as they were presented, and two when repeating them in reverse (Cutting 1985, p.210). Second, the information may be presented visually: a number of letters are projected on to a screen, and the subject is required to say how many are present (Neale *et al.* 1969). Several authors have demonstrated reduced attention span in schizophrenia (Hinton and Withers 1971; Spohn, Thetford and Woodham 1970).[35] Others, however, have found a better-than-normal attention span for visual information in people with the acute form of the condition (Cegalis, Leen and Solomon 1977) and a normal span in those with the chronic form, at least when they are not subject to distractions (Neale *et al.* 1969).

One might expect more unanimity with regard to the ability to selectively attend. One author argues that people with schizophrenia fail to 'segmentalize' life's experiences correctly: 'If there is any creature who can be accused of not seeing the forest for the trees,' he observes, 'it is the schizophrenic' (Shakow 1950, p.388). In fact, careful research in this area has shown no impairment of selective attention, at least when information is presented aurally. Schneider (1976) asked a group of people with schizophrenia to follow a passage in one ear, first with no distraction, and then with one of five distractions playing in the other. These distractions were a quiet noise, a loud noise, someone reading about physics, someone describing the history of the hospital in which the experiment was taking place and someone talking about the precise content of the subject's delusions. Only with respect to the last of these did their ability to attend selectively deteriorate, suggesting that the attention deficit was related only to their concerns regarding their delusions and was not a general phenomenon (see Cutting 1985, p.213, for a discussion). When information is presented visually, however, there is some evidence that people with schizophrenia perform worse than others in tests of selective attention.[36]

With regard to the ability to shift attention from one subject to another, however, people with schizophrenia are markedly worse than others. In the Wisconsin Card-Sorting Test the subject is presented with four playing cards which differ from each other in each of three respects: the nature of the symbol they depict (circles, crosses, stars and triangles); colour; and the number of each symbol shown (one, two, three or four). He is then required to sort the remaining cards. The task is to establish by trial and error whether he is required to sort according to the nature of the symbol, its colour or the number of each symbol shown. He is guided only by the examiner's comments of 'right' or 'wrong' after each card is laid down. The examiner periodically changes the criterion by which the cards should be sorted without telling the subject. When the criterion changes, normal subjects make several mistakes before working out, for instance, that the cards are no longer to be sorted according to colour and are now to be sorted according to symbol. People with chronic schizophrenia take longer to establish this (Fey 1951).

This inappropriate repetition of a previous response is usually called 'perseveration'. As such, it is more frequently described in association with the so-called 'organic' psychiatric conditions such as dementia. It is particularly likely to occur in those forms of dementia, such as Pick's disease, where the frontal lobes are primarily affected. It may also occur where the damage to the frontal lobes comes from other sources. Milner (1963) found that performance on the Wisconsin Card-Sorting Test was impaired in subjects who had parts of their frontal lobes removed as treatment for epilepsy. Surgically induced lesions in other areas of the brain had no comparable effect. Similar findings have been recorded when the frontal lobe damage is a result of head injury (see Drewe 1973; Lishman 1978, p.150).

Teuber (1964) conducted more subtle testing of the cognitive deficits consequent upon frontal lobe damage. His subjects did badly when asked to draw a vertical line while leaning over; when they were vertical, they performed as well as controls. They were also unable to touch the part of their own body corresponding to the part marked on a drawing. Teuber's interpretation of these results was that, while his subjects were able to anticipate events, they could not picture themselves as agents of those events. Hence they could describe the consequences of leaning over, but could not adapt their drawing to take these consequences into account. He argued that specific deficits in attention which result from damage to the frontal lobe of the brain affect what he called the 'will' which, he argued, involved an appreciation of the consequences of actions and of one's own role in producing those consequences. Luria reached similar conclusions. In his scheme, any action involved the continuous comparing of a plan of action with what has been achieved so far. This process allowed the control of one's own acts and was interfered with by frontal lobe damage (see Luria 1980, pp.246–365; Luria and Homskaya 1964; Luria, Karpov and Yarbuss 1966).

ABNORMAL MENTAL STATES AND THE PROVISION OF EXCUSES

It was argued in Chapter 2 that an excuse exists where the actor's capacity or opportunity to choose has been compromised. It may also be that excuses prevent an inference from a criminal act to the character of the actor, although, it was argued earlier, this might better be described as a consequence of many excuses rather than their defining characteristic (see p.38). In the first part of this chapter the effects of psychiatric conditions on the various mental faculties have been described. Many of these conditions reduce the actor's capacity and opportunity to choose. The extent to which they do so, however, varies.

The first cause of this variation is that the mental faculties are affected relatively, rather than absolutely, by the conditions described here. Consciousness has been described as existing on a continuum between full alertness and coma (see p.64). Clearly, a subject cannot be held responsible for acts or omissions conducted while comatose.[37] Equally, he cannot expect to be excused on account of having slept poorly the night before he pulled the trigger. But the ground between these two extremes, in terms of being held responsible, is less clearly marked. There is no obvious point on the continuum of consciousness where responsibility could be said to begin. Similarly, the pathological changes seen in Alzheimer's disease, the commonest form of dementia, differ in degree but not in kind from the changes associated with normal ageing.[38] The same can be said for the intellectual changes. Normal ageing does not excuse crime: at what point should dementia? In addition, intellectual function can fluctuate in the course of a dementing illness (Lishman 1978, p.537). Nor are delusions simply present or absent. They may vary in intensity (Garety and Helmsley 1987) and, intriguingly, may be associated with an awareness that the belief is 'abnormal' and a sign of illness. This phenomenon, called insight, does not necessarily increase as patients improve and disappear as they relapse (McEvoy et al. 1989). Should deluded people be excused by the presence of an abnormal belief influencing their actions or by their lack of insight into the abnormal nature of that belief?

Second, the various mental faculties described here affect each other. Thus a lowering of one's level of consciousness interferes both with one's perception and with one's ability to attend. Emotional changes also affect the way one sees things, and profound depression interferes with thinking to a degree that can mimic dementia. Particularly with respect to the eye injuries described on p.70, it is clear that the behavioural effects of changes in thinking and feeling can amount to more than the sum of the parts (see also the discussion of the adequacy of delusional motivation on p.69). They may also amount to less, as when seemingly important changes in belief are not accompanied by a change in behaviour.[39] In addition to the difficulties, described above, of quantifying elements such as consciousness, there is the problem of assessing the strength of these various interactions.

A third problem is that some of the mental-state changes outlined in the first part of the chapter are under a degree of voluntary control. The difficulty of distinguishing some of the dissociative states from the conscious mimicry of psychiatric symptoms has already been described (see p.66). Some have suggested, however, that too much emphasis has been given to the supposed dichotomy between malingering and the presentation of 'genuine' symptoms.[40] Kretschmer, who treated dissociative states in wartime, held that they were an instinctive reaction to protect the individual against stress. He also held, however, that they could be prolonged either through a non-specific habit-forming mechanism or by a conscious appreciation of the benefits of remaining 'unwell' (Kretschmer 1961, pp.67–78). One reviewer refers to a continuum of clinical phenomena between awareness and unconscious motivation (see Merskey 1979, p.82) while some studies of dissociative fugue emphasise that sufferers are often, to a variable extent, aware of what is happening to them.[41]

The final reason why it is difficult to quantify the effect of psychiatric conditions on an actor's capacity and opportunity to choose relates to Gestalt psychology. This school was advanced in the first half of the twentieth century by the German psychiatrists Max Wertheimer (1945), Kurt Koffka (1950) and Wolfgang Kohler. They held that the brain organised the world according to a few simple principles. One of these is the distinction between 'figure' and 'ground', where 'figure' refers to anything which we may wish to concentrate on and 'ground' to the mass of other information which is available. We analyse visual information according to criteria such as the proximity to each other of the objects we are looking at (Banks and Prinzmetal 1976) and whether or not they exhibit an unbroken contour (Prinzmetal and Banks 1977). In other words, patterns matter. They allow us to recognise what we have learned to be important. Similarly with sounds: four drumbeats with a pause between the second and third are heard as two pairs, and rapid sequences of notes are grouped according to their pitch by subjects attempting to remember them (Bregman and Campbell 1971).

These observations could be explained using earlier principles of psychology, such as association learning. We might recognise patterns because their component parts occur together so frequently. What Gestalt psychology added that was new was the suggestion that there was a pressure to fit experience into patterns, not simply a willingness to accept these patterns if they appear. Koffka (1950) described this as the 'law of pregnance' (p.110). When we read the first two lines of a syllogism such as 'All men are mortal. Caius is a man. Therefore Caius is mortal,' (see Merskey 1979, p.82) we do not usually react with indifference. We examine them to see if they lead logically to the third. As one author put it, describing Newton's thoughts on watching the apple fall, 'the mental gap called for closure' (Katz 1951, p.88). The phenomenon being described is not so very different from the, presumably apocryphal, tale of communication in the First World War. Simple lack of clarity could explain the loss of the meaning of, 'Send reinforcements, we are going to advance.' But a willingness to create sense out of what was being heard would be required for the conveyance of, 'Send three and fourpence, we are going to a dance.'

People with schizophrenia have difficulty distinguishing figure from ground (Straube 1975). As one author put it 'The clouds of essential properties, which every object holds within itself, have been set free' (Conrad 1958; translated by Cutting 1985, p.372). They categorise poorly, particularly with respect to emotive issues (see p.72), and make 'clang associations', moving from one train of thought to another because of the verbal similarity of key words (Hamilton 1985, p.39). It may also be that the patterns into which we seek to fit our perceptions are altered by schizophrenia. Gestalt psychology suggests that a relatively small perceptual error might have large behavioural consequences as a result of the pressure to fit experience into these patterns.

SUMMARY

If psychiatric conditions are to be grounds for exculpation, they must impair the sufferer's ability to choose. There are many ways in which they may do this. Consciousness may be impaired, so that the subject is unaware of the circumstances in which he finds himself, or of the likely consequences of what he is doing. His emotional state may be altered, so that he wishes things that he would not otherwise wish or views things in a way that he would not normally view them. He may find himself driven to act in ways which he would not when healthy, although, it has been argued, whether such impulses should be described as irresistible is doubtful. His perception may be distorted so that he sees and hears things differently. His ability to think clearly may be impaired and the content of his thoughts may be altered by such conditions as manic-depression and schizophrenia.

Unfortunately, identifying the mental-state changes which can diminish an actor's capacity to choose is easier than identifying the point at which that actor can no longer be said to be responsible. First, most of the changes described here are matters of degree, ranging from minor impairment to total loss of function. Second, the changes interact with each other, often in idiosyncratic ways, so that even if it was possible to accurately quantify, say, consciousness, it would be impossible to name a point at which an actor should be held responsible. A trivial level of conscious impairment might lead to the misidentification of a bystander's umbrella as a weapon and hence to an assault. Third, the degree to which psychiatric symptoms are the subject of insight and under voluntary control varies considerably. Finally, the influence of relatively minor impairments can be disproportionate, given our tendency to look for patterns in the world around us. The next chapter will examine those tests of responsibility which have been developed in England and Wales and in the United States, and discuss the degree to which these problems have been addressed.

NOTES

1.   'The capacities in question are those of understanding, reasoning and control of conduct' (Hart 1968, p.227).

2.   The term 'consciousness' is being used here in the medical sense to refer to an awareness of the self and of the environment (see Gelder *et al.* 1983, p.28). Philosophers also use the term, but with different emphases. To Locke, consciousness was inseparable from thinking and, since thinking permitted reflection, represented the central component of personal identity (see Locke 1690,

p.335). To Descartes, consciousness, and, in particular, consciousness of our own thoughts, is the only way we know things exist (Descartes 1637, p.127; for a review see Klein 1984).

3. Such an effect is subtle: people with schizophrenia do not usually appear drowsy.

4. The term 'cycloid psychosis' was introduced by Kleist (1928) to denote psychoses which were neither schizophrenic nor manic-depressive. Leonhard (1957) described three types, all of which are held to carry a good prognosis and all of which are 'bipolar' in the sense that the sufferer may exhibit either of two contrasting constellations of symptoms. Thus in 'anxiety-happiness psychosis' the symptoms are primarily those of a change of mood, towards either nervousness or elation. 'Motility psychosis', involves becoming more or less active. Perplexity is said to be a symptom of 'confusion psychosis', a condition marked by abnormality in the form of the patient's thoughts, and where the bipolarity lies between excitement and underactivity. See also Perris (1974).

5. Hamilton (1985, p.82) refers to the subject feeling that he is not his 'normal, natural self'.

6. Hwu *et al.* (1981), however, found the related phenomenon of derealisation in over 40 per cent of people with schizophrenia. That the experimental findings are inconsistent may be due to the range of definitions of depersonalisation available.

7. The original description was by Mayer-Gross (1924).

8. Kendell and Zealley's assertion (1993, p.515) that the different personalities remain unaware of each other is at variance with some of the older descriptions of the condition (see Prince 1905; Thigpen and Cleckley 1957).

9. In a foretaste of descriptions of multiple personality, James comments: 'Mr. Bourne's skull today still covers two distinct personal selves' (1891, p.392).

10. See also Stengel (1943): 'The condition seems nowadays to occur in the textbooks only ... in reading reports one cannot help feeling that some of them succeeded in deceiving the psychiatrist as well as the police' (p.226).

11. French and Shechmeister (1983) argue that one of their cases, whose *alter* personality was that of a thief, failed both limbs of the Californian test of insanity, based on the American Law Institute's *Model Penal Code* (Article 4.07). Through ignorance of what was going on, the 'primary' personality neither appreciated the criminality of his conduct nor was able to conform his conduct to the law.

12. Although the author does not give details (see Abrams 1983).

13. Gunn and Taylor (1993, pp.65–66) contrast somnambulistic, unconscious acts, where the actor's motivation is usually unintelligible, with those described in association with multiple personality:

> In cases where the defence of multiple personality is advanced, the motivation is usually clear. The activities leading up to it are complex, extended over time and goal directed. Frequently no documented history exists prior to the offending of the multiple personality disorder which comes to light only after being charged with the offence (p.66).

The warning, regarding the hazards of allowing a criminal act to become the evidence of a previously unsuspected psychiatric condition, has been echoed elsewhere (Fenwick 1990, p.284). Maudsley (1897) states: 'Now if it were possible in all cases of homicidal insanity to point to evidence of derangement before the outbreak, there would be infinitely less disinclination to admit the existence of disease' (p.166).

14. Even psychiatrists sympathetic to the notion of an unconsciously generated multiple personality report that some patients withhold crucial information (see, for instance, Kluft 1987, p.368).

15. See Gunn and Taylor (1993, p.431); the example which the authors provide is that of an arson attack.

16. The reasoning behind this suggested compromise would only apply in the United Kingdom, however. The authors argue that multiple personality reduces self-control. In some parts of the United States this could offer grounds for an insanity defence (see Chapter 5).

17. For a discussion of the philosophy of action see McGinn (1979). For a discussion of the applicability of psychiatric factors see Buchanan (1993).

18.   The issue of the classification of depression is a complex one: some people who have only ever been depressed are said to suffer from manic-depression because the particular symptoms which they experience raise the possibility that a manic episode will follow. The condition can be defined according to several different parameters: the nature of the present episode (depressive or manic); the course of the condition – unipolar, indicating that the nature of each episode is the same, and bipolar, indicating that the person has experienced, or is likely to experience, episodes of both depression and mania; and the cause (reactive or endogenous). The waters are further muddied by attempts to include further detailed descriptions of the subject's symptoms, hence 'neurotic depression' and 'psychotic depression'. For present purposes, the terms 'depression' and 'mania' will be used to describe an abnormally lowered or raised mood (see Gelder et al. 1983, pp.194–200).

19.   In other words, where the mental component of the crime amounts to negligence, or perhaps that form of recklessness (stemming from R. v. Caldwell) which requires proof only that there was an obvious risk which the defendant should have considered.

20.   The explanation, according to Schipkowensky, lies in the 'pathologically increased social connections' of people with mania (1968, p.63).

21.   It is not clear why so many reports of self-harm involve eye injuries. It may be that the metaphorical and religious significance attached to the eye makes it particularly vulnerable. It may also be that such injuries are seldom fatal and present a particular challenge to a surgeon. Most of the reports appear in the ophthalmology press and the emphasis is on surgical treatment rather than psychiatric phenomenology.

22.   Hafner and Boker (1973) found that 56 per cent of killers with an affective psychosis showed delusions at the time of their offence. In a control group of subjects with an affective psychosis who had not acted violently, the proportion with delusions was 26 per cent.

23.   The term 'distortion' is being used here in a non-technical sense. The concept of 'cognitive distortion', however, is central to some theories of the aetiology and treatment of depression (see Beck et al. 1979). By these theories, depression is caused by a persistent misinterpretation of the significance of often mundane events. Thus a personal achievement will be downgraded by the thought, 'but anyone could have done that'. Treatment then requires the therapist to assist the patient in exposing such assumptions to the light of reason.

24.   For a description of the effect of mood on reasoning dating from the first half of the nineteenth century see Abercrombie (1833).

25.   Wulach's sample was the largest and his findings may therefore carry more weight. For a review see Gunn and Taylor (1993, p.348).

26.   Maudsley, an advocate of irresistible impulses, was sceptical of the notion that such impulses could exist in the absence of other mental-state changes:

> In most cases [of impulsive insanity] I believe it will be found, on an intimate knowledge of the person's feelings and doings, that there is more derangement than appears on the surface. His whole mental tone is more or less affected, so that his feelings are blunted or changed, the natural interests of life extinguished, and his judgements of his relations to others and of their relations to him somewhat impaired; he is apt to become suspicious of and hostile to those who have been his nearest friends and acquaintances, and may finally get delusions concerning them. (Maudsley 1897, p.163)

27.   'A person is said to labor under a hallucination, or to be a visionary, who has a thorough conviction of the perception of a sensation, when no external object, suited to excite this sensation, has impressed the senses' (Esquirol 1845, p.93). Esquirol has been criticised on the grounds that his definition fails to cover the so-called functional hallucinations, where a normal sound, such as the ticking of a clock, precipitates a hallucination, such as a man's voice (see Hamilton 1985, p.19). In fact, Esquirol's requirement, that the stimulus be 'suited to excite' the perception, would seem to take care of this objection.

28.   This is sometimes described as 'an obsessive desire for sameness'. This phrase, employed by Kanner in his original description, is now regarded as unsatisfactory; the symptomatology is not the same as that of OCD.

29. This was first described in German by Asperger (1944) and entered the English-speaking literature with Van Krevelen's paper (1971).

30. Although children with Asperger's syndrome speak better than those with autism they may, when
young, display the same tendency to reverse pronouns (Bosch 1962, p.130).

31. The term, and its relatives, have been employed – confusingly and often interchangeably – for
many years. 'Psychopathic personality' is a term in more common usage, but is avoided here
because of its technical function as a category of mental disorder in the Mental Health Act in
England and Wales (for reviews of the topic see Gunn and Robertson 1976; Pichot 1978).

32. 'Its outline will not be firm until much more is known about its genetics, psychopathology and
neuropathology' (Lewis 1974, p.139).

33. Blackburn (1988) argues that deviations from normal personality and deviations from the norms
of social behaviour belong to different 'universes of discourse' (p.511). Antisocial personality is a
fatally flawed category because it seeks to invoke elements of both. A similar line is adopted by
Elliot (1991). Holmes (1991) is more radical, contending that 'psychopathy' is a term which be-
longs to the field of ethics, not medicine.

34. This is the standard definition which psychiatrists are expected to abide by (Gelder et al. 1983,
pp.12–19). Most would acknowledge its inadequacies. For example, a seemingly outlandish
belief may turn out to be true. This would not stop psychiatrists from regarding it as a delusion if it
seemed an unreasonable thing for the patient to believe.

35. The study by Spohn et al. (1970) is one of the few in this area in which patients' medication was
stopped. Researchers (e.g. Cegalis et al. 1977; Neale et al. 1969) more commonly test patients on
drugs. An attempt is then made to correlate dose and test performance for the whole sample. If no
such correlation is found, impairments in test performance are assumed to be unrelated to
medication.

36. Fonseca et al. (1978) presented a group of people with schizophrenia with a red or yellow light.
The yellow light, they were informed, was of no significance. The red light indicated that they
would receive an electric shock if they failed to depress a button. Normal subjects rapidly pressed
the button when they saw the red light. People with schizophrenia also did this, but did the same
thing in response to the yellow light. The authors concluded that people with schizophrenia were
failing to selectively attend. Another interpretation would be that they saw no reason to take
chances.

37. Unless he was to blame for being in that state; self-induced intoxication does not usually excuse
criminal acts. This issue will be discussed further in the next chapter.

38. 'All of the changes that have been described in association with senile dementia ... were seen in
some measure in the brains of non-demented subjects. In other words, the differences appear to be
of a quantitative rather than qualitative nature' (Roth 1971, p.5. See also Gelder et al. 1983,
p.507).

39. 'Often, indeed, belief and conduct are completely divorced from one another, or, even,
grotesquely inconsistent. Thus, the "Queen of the World" will contentedly carry out her daily task
of scrubbing the ward floor, and the omnipotent millionaire will beg plaintively for a small gift of
tobacco' (Hart 1912, p.33).

40. See, for instance, Lishman on the feigning of dementia: 'Thus even the stimulant may have a
partial self-deception, with the result that the boundaries between fully conscious feigning of dementia and hysterical pseudodementia are probably far from definite, and the two will be inextri-
cably mixed in many cases' (1978, p.570).

41. Stengel (1943) states: 'In the great majority of cases with wandering states the patients are at some
stage of the wandering condition aware of the urge to wander and keep moving' (p.225). He does
not then address whether they are able to do anything about the urge.

CHAPTER 5

What Does the Law Allow to Excuse?

The previous chapter examined ways in which psychiatric conditions contribute to the provision of excuses. This chapter will examine the mechanisms by which those excuses are accommodated by Anglo-American criminal law. These mechanisms are several. The oldest examples of exculpation consequent upon a defendant's mental state led to the development of what is now known on both sides of the Atlantic as the 'insanity defence'. A related doctrine – unhelpfully labelled 'irresistible impulse' – has a history which intertwines with that of the insanity defence, and which has exerted considerable influence on legislation in the United States.

The United States has also seen the adoption of an alternative to the traditional doctrine of insanity. This is referred to here and elsewhere as the 'product test'. Also reviewed will be the defence of automatism. Finally, the offence of infanticide will be described. A conviction of infanticide has the same effect as a finding of guilty of manslaughter. Diminished responsibility also reduces what would otherwise be murder to manslaughter, but can only be introduced once the defendant has been charged with murder; it was discussed with mitigation (p.54). Infanticide is dealt with here because it stands as a piece of legislation in its own right and can be charged by the Crown in the first instance.

INSANITY

The earliest references to excusing the insane in England and Wales have been assembled by Walker (1968). One text, which dates from no later than the start of the eleventh century, and which may have been written by Egbert, the eighth-century Archbishop of York, contains an injunction to make special provision when killings are committed by the mentally disordered: 'If a man fall out of his senses or wits, and it come to pass that he kill someone, let his kinsmen pay for the victim, and preserve the slayer against all else of that kind' (see Thorpe 1840; translated by Walker 1968, p.15).

The first medieval English jurist, Bracton, writing in the middle of the thirteenth century, defined the criteria which, in his opinion, were to be employed when establishing guilt or innocence:

> For a crime is not committed unless the will to harm is present. Misdeeds are distinguished both by will and intention [and theft is not committed without the thought of thieving]. And then there is what can be said about the child and the madman, for the one is protected by his innocence of design, the other by the misfortune of his deed. In misdeeds we look to the will and not the outcome. (1640; translated by Walker 1968, p.26).

Bracton is here emphasising the insane offender's reasons for acting as he did.[1] It was to be 600 years, however, before the M'Naghten Rules led to the incorporation of the offender's reasons into English law. Until then, instead of seeking to understand the defendant's motivation, the courts were more concerned with his general condition.

To this end, at least from the Middle Ages, a broad distinction was made between two forms of mental incapacity, one present from birth and the other acquired later in life.[2] The former is usually referred to in the older literature as 'idiocy', and is the forerunner of the 'mental subnormality' and 'severe mental subnormality' categories of the Mental Health Act 1983. The latter is usually described as 'lunacy' or 'madness'.

By the middle of the seventeenth century, however, a second important distinction had emerged. This lay between complete and partial insanity. Matthew Hale, the Lord Chief Justice of England, wrote:

> There is a partial insanity of mind…; some persons that have a competent use of reason in respect of some subjects, are yet under a particular dementia in respect of some particular discourses, subjects or applications; or else it is partial in respect of degrees; and this is the condition of very many, especially melancholy persons, who for the most part discover their defect in excessive fears and griefs, and yet are not wholly destitute of the use of reason. (Hale 1736, p.30)[3]

Hale made considerable play of the distinction between partial and complete insanity, for it was this, and not that between partial insanity and mental well-being, which determined whether or not the defendant could be punished. The reasons for this are not clear. Hale himself wrote that most criminals were suffering from some degree of partial insanity when they committed crimes. It may be that he feared that many 'ordinary criminals' would be released if partial insanity were allowed to excuse.

How was the presence or absence of insanity, complete or partial, to be judged? Throughout the period from Bracton to Hale, it was left to the jury to decide.[4] In 1723, however, at the trial of Arnold,[5] Mr Justice Tracy offered what was to become known as the 'Wild Beast Test': 'It is not every kind of frantic humour, or something unaccountable in a man's actions, that points him out to be such a madman as is to be exempted from punishment: it must be a man that is totally deprived of his understanding and memory, and doth not know what he is doing, no more than an infant, than a brute, or a wild beast' (*R. v. Arnold* at 764, 765). Maudsley was to contrast the exacting standard applied by this test to that which applied in civil cases. A man who was not thought fit to take care of himself and his affairs could still be hung on the basis that, at the time of the crime, he was less than 'totally deprived of his understanding' (Maudsley 1897, p.97).

It is not clear, however, that such strict criteria were applied even at the time. Walker describes the trial in 1731 of Edward Stafford when an acquittal on grounds of insanity was permitted although the evidence was inconsistent with a total deprivation of understanding (Walker 1968, pp.57–58). Certainly, there is ample evidence that by the beginning of the nineteenth century the courts were dissatisfied with the stringency of Tracy's test. At the trial of Hadfield[6] in 1800, the Attorney General's assertion that acquittal required a total deprivation of memory and understanding was rebutted by the defendant's counsel, Lord Erskine, on the grounds that 'no such madness ever existed in the world' (*R. v. Hadfield* at 1312). Erskine argued that his client suffered from delusions and that this alone was sufficient to render him legally insane. Hadfield was acquitted. It was only in the wake of this trial that the vexed question of what to do with those who were insane when they committed their crime was finally settled. The court had publicly debated what was to be done with Hadfield. With the passing of the Act of 1800 'For the Safe Custody of Insane Persons Charged with Offences' (39 and 40 George III, c.94) the correct procedure became the passing of a special verdict,[7] which made clear the reasons for the finding of not guilty and which allowed detention 'until His Majesty's pleasure be known'.

It is not clear that the outcome of Hadfield's trial represented a relaxation of the restrictive criteria for insanity rather than a triumph of his counsel's oration. The case of Bellingham of 1812,[8] however, did allow students of psychiatric jurisprudence to comment upon the judicial criteria. Lord Mansfield, the Chief Justice, charged the jury that, in order to be found not guilty on the grounds of insanity, the defendant should be incapable of distinguishing right from wrong (see Russell 1819, p.16). It might be supposed that this test would have met with more approval from the alienists than did that outlined by Tracy, if only because it encouraged a more sophisticated analysis of mental function than was required by the so-called 'Wild Beast Test'. Not so. Ray (1839) complained, in terms which echoed those employed by Lord Erskine in Hadfield's trial, that the logical consequence of Lord Mansfield's charge to the jury was that 'no man can ever successfully plead insanity' (p.29). Ray argued that, while insanity could produce signs and symptoms which lead directly to the commission of a criminal act, in other respects the appreciation of right and wrong was usually unaffected.[9]

That none of the criteria which have been discussed here had achieved pre-eminence by the time Daniel M'Naghten killed Drummond, Robert Peel's secretary, is evident from the fact that most of them were invoked in the course of his trial (R. v. M'Naghten). M'Naghten had acted in the belief that the Tories were spying on him; his trial took place in 1843. The Solicitor-General, prosecuting, drawing attention to the rationality of much of M'Naghten's behaviour in the period leading up to the shooting to demonstrate that his insanity could be no more than partial, quoted Matthew Hale in dismissing the notion that the partially insane were to be excused (see p.85). He further followed Hale's argument, without quoting him, in asserting that few crimes were committed by normal people, but that this did not mean that the perpetrators should go free.[10] Defence counsel, Alexander Cockburn, made use of Erskine's contention[11] that the presence of delusions was the true mark of insanity. At the end of his submission, however, he introduced a new set of criteria; namely, that his client was not only suffering from a delusion but was also incapable of doing other than acting on it by killing the man whom he believed to be the leader of his persecutors.[12] This last twist was a curious addition. If Cockburn's contention was that the presence of delusions was the true sign of madness, it is not clear why he should have wished to argue additionally that his client had no choice but to act on his beliefs. He may have been attempting to erect a second line of defence in case the presence of delusions was not seen as contradicting the prosecution's suggestion that M'Naghten was only partially insane. Finally, the Chief Justice indicated that in his view the correct test of insanity was that which had been described by Lord Mansfield (see p.86); namely, whether or not the accused was capable of distinguishing right from wrong. The jury, if they followed the advice of the Chief Justice, decided that he was not. They returned a special verdict, and M'Naghten was removed to the Bethlem Hospital.

In the wake of the verdict, the government came under pressure to clarify the procedure relating to insanity in criminal trials.[13] The House of Lords summoned the English judges to answer five questions. The fifth concerned the appropriate-ness, or otherwise, of medical witnesses giving evidence when they had not interviewed the defendant. In response to the first and fourth questions, the judges stated that in cases of partial insanity the defendant should be treated as if his delusional beliefs were correct (R. v. M'Naghten at 211). It was in response to the second and third, which related to the standards by which insanity was to be judged and the way in which the question was to be presented to the jury, that they offered the criteria which have become known as the M'Naghten Rules. To establish a defence of insanity it was necessary that 'the accused was labouring under such a defect of reason, from disease of the mind, as not to know the nature and quality of the act he was doing; or, if he did know it, that he did not know he was doing what was wrong' (R. v. M'Naghten at 210). Ironically, as Walker has pointed out, if these criteria had been strictly applied at his trial, M'Naghten would not have been acquitted (1968, p.102).

In England and Wales, the ensuing 150 years have seen little change in the criteria used at law to measure sanity. This has not been for lack of suggestions. In the nineteenth century, doctors argued that the M'Naghten Rules were too cognitive and made no allowance for the insane defendant whose intellectual function was preserved but whose ability to control his behaviour was nevertheless impaired (see Maudsley 1897; Prichard 1842; Ray 1839 and the next section). Fitzjames Stephen agreed. He suggested: 'It ought to be the law of England that no act is a crime if the person who does it is, at the time when it is done, prevented either by defective mental power or by any disease affecting his mind from controlling his own conduct, unless the absence of control has been produced by his own default' (1883, p.168).[14] In 1924 the Atkin Committee recommended that the M'Naghten Rules should be kept but that, in addition, the insanity defence should be available when the act 'is committed under an impulse which the prisoner was by mental disease in substance deprived of any power to resist' (Committee on Insanity and Crime 1924, p.21). In 1953 the Gowers Commission made a similar suggestion.[15]

Only the Butler Committee, of the authoritative scrutineers of the insanity defence, failed to recommend the inclusion of a clause referring to the power to control one's actions (Committee on Mentally Abnormal Offenders 1975, p.227). They had less reason to do so, however, because their own suggested alternative would have been available to anyone who could be shown on the balance of probabilities to suffer from 'severe mental illness'. Many defendants whose ability to control their actions was impaired by illness could be expected to avail themselves of this. The Committee's proposals were adopted by the Law Commission and included in their proposals for more widespread reform of the criminal law (1989, volume 2, pp.220–226).

The reasons why none of these recommendations have been adopted are not obvious. In the case of the proposals made by the Butler Committee, the competing demands on parliamentary time may have contributed. Another explanation is certainly the reduced importance of the insanity defence now that the partial defence of diminished responsibility is available when the charge is one of murder (see p.54). A further contributing factor may be that the abolition of capital punishment has rendered the issue less pressing.

In the United States, alternatives to the M'Naghten Rules have made more progress. There were a number of contradictions in the judges' replies to the House of Lords' questions. As described above (see p.87), the judges identified two sets of criteria by which the defendant's legal sanity was to be assessed. The first concerned whether the defendant made what amounts to a 'mistake of fact': if he was labouring under a 'partial delusion only' (R. v. M'Naghten at 211), he was to be treated as if his delusional beliefs were true. The second concerned whether or not the defendant knew the nature of what he was doing and the difference between right and wrong. The judges gave no indication as to which set of criteria should take priority (see Guttmacher and Weihofen 1952, p.416). The issue is of little importance in England and Wales, where the first set of criteria are no longer used (see Williams 1961, p.442).[16] But in the United States, several jurisdictions initially employed the 'mistake of fact' criteria. The results were described in one appellate case as 'inhumane' (State v. Jones at 250). A defendant who was psychotic when he acted was liable to be convicted unless a delusion could be shown to have caused the behaviour in question. Even a delusional threat could not contribute to a defence if the defendant's action was disproportionately violent.

At the end of the nineteenth century, Davis v. United States provided a federal rule whereby a defendant could be excused: '...though conscious of [the nature of the act] and able to distinguish between right and wrong, ...yet his will...has been otherwise than voluntarily so completely destroyed that his actions are not subject to it, but are beyond his control' (at 378). Many states adopted similar criteria, and the insanity defence consisted of a knowledge test derived from M'Naghten with or without this 'irresistible impulse' addition until the middle of the twentieth century. In 1962 the American Law Institute included a clause in their Model Penal Code which made reference to both knowledge and volition. A person was not responsible for criminal conduct if, 'at the time of such conduct, as the result of mental disease or defect he lacks the substantial capacity either to appreciate the criminality [wrongfulness] of his conduct or to conform his conduct to the requirements of the law' (p.66). The American Law Institute's proposals met with general approval and were widely adopted by the states. The shooting of Ronald Reagan by John Hinckley, however, and Hinckley's successful use of an insanity defence which employed these criteria, generated objections that they were over-inclusive.

Partly as a result of the Hinckley verdict, the 1980s saw various changes to the insanity defence in the United States (see Mackay 1988). Montana, Idaho and Utah abolished the defence entirely, leaving the requirements of mens rea to 'carry the freight', in Norval Morris' phrase, of excusing the mentally ill (Morris 1982, p.65). Other states introduced a new verdict, one of 'guilty but mentally ill'. This was intended to cater for people who were not legally insane but who were nevertheless mentally ill at the time they offended. It allowed a prison disposal (South Dakota and Pennsylvania are examples; for a review see Slobogin 1985). Still others left the test of insanity unchanged but transferred the burden of proving that insanity to the defendant (Arizona, Colorado and Connecticut, among others).[17] In Hinckley's case it had lain with the prosecution. Finally, several states – Texas and Indiana, for instance – reverted to tests of insanity which omit any 'control' element, and which, in their cognitive emphasis, are very similar to the M'Naghten Rules.[18]

If the insanity defence in England and Wales has not been subject to the same changes in substance, considerable legal energy has still been expended in refining and defining the answers which the judges offered in response to the House of Lords' questions. When they referred to knowledge, on the defendant's part, that what he was doing was wrong, they intended that this should mean morally wrong.[19]

There are at least two varieties of knowledge of moral wrongness, however. On the one hand, one may know that one's act would be disapproved of by most people. On the other, one may believe that one should not engage in it. Many terrorists presumably possess the first and lack the second. Which meaning is the more important? Courts in the United States have on different occasions adopted both.[20] In New Zealand the jury are instructed: 'The meaning to be given to that phrase is the meaning which is commonly accepted' (*R. v. Macmillan* at 622). In England, the distinction does not arise. The courts have concluded, after a half-hearted dalliance with a moral interpretation,[21] that wrong means against the law (*R. v. Windle* at 2).[22] The issue is of some importance. Fifty per cent of defences which employ the insanity defence in England and Wales do so by addressing the wrongness limb of the M'Naghten Rules (Mackay 1990), despite the view of some that this limb adds nothing to the substance of the defence (see Williams 1983, p.645).

What of the 'nature and quality of the act'? In Canada the consequences of an act are considered part of its 'nature and quality' (*R. v. O* at 155). Similarly in China, where the physical nature of an act is taken to include an appreciation of the 'surrounding environment' and the 'socially harmful nature' (Yang 1993). In England and Wales, by contrast, the 'nature and quality' of the act has been restricted to its physical character (*R. v. Codere* at 27) and does not include the consequences (*R. v. Dickie* at 178).[23] Courts in the United States have similarly eschewed the opportunity to apply a broad definition to 'nature and quality' (Goldstein 1967, pp.50, 51). It has been argued that the narrow interpretation adopted by the courts in England and Wales is illogical and contrary to the principles of *mens rea* (McAuley 1993, p.28). This assumes that the insanity defence operates according to such principles, a far-from-secure assumption (see Bonnie and Slobogin 1980; Morse 1979; Walker 1968, pp.40, 81).[24]

It might be supposed that the greatest difficulty would attend the use of the term 'disease of the mind'. After all, medical writers have struggled with the definition of mental disease.[25] One possible solution was ruled out when the courts made clear that it did not mean 'disease of the brain' (see Smith and Hogan 1996, p.203).[26] Those who write from a legal perspective usually include the psychoses but exclude the neuroses (Goldstein 1967, p.48) and the personality disorders (Royal Commission on Capital Punishment 1953, p.139). In fact, the courts are less rigid than this. Between 1975 and 1988, of 49 successful insanity defences run in England and Wales, three defendants had a diagnosis of personality disorder and 51 of alcohol or drug abuse (Mackay 1990). In the United States, similarly, personality disorder and substance abuse are both used as evidence of disease of the mind (McGreevy, Steadman and Callahan 1991). Indeed, the American courts have rejected the notion that the availability of the insanity defence should depend on a defendant belonging to one of a number of diagnostic categories (*Carter* v. *United States* at 617).

The definition of disease of the mind has generated little debate in the appellate courts when the question has been whether or not the defendant should be found guilty. By contrast, when it is accepted that the defendant is not guilty and the question is whether the defence amounts to insanity or sane automatism, the definition of disease of the mind has generated a large body of case law (reviewed on pp.98 *et seq.*). Sane automatism results in a simple acquittal, whereas the range of sentencing options following a finding of not guilty by reason of insanity includes indefinite detention in hospital.

The most likely explanation for the relative lack of discussion of the meaning of disease of the mind when the issue is one of exculpation is that the courts have adopted the position suggested by Mr Justice Devlin in *R.* v. *Kemp* (at 129). Devlin argued that the term 'disease of the mind' existed only to make it clear that the 'defect of reason' could not simply be the product of bad upbringing. In other respects, any psychological condition could count as a disease of the mind, provided it generated a lack of knowledge. The Criminal Procedure (Insanity and Unfitness to Plead) Act 1991 removed the requirement that the defendant be admitted to hospital following a verdict of insanity (see p.99). If the number of defendants pleading insanity increases as a result of the Act, there may be a corresponding increase in the attention paid to the legal meaning of 'disease of the mind'.

IRRESISTIBLE IMPULSE

We have seen that one forensic psychiatrist, in a recent review of irresistible impulse, finds it difficult to see how the concept has survived for so long (see Mawson 1990). It might be better to ask why the term, rather than the concept, has demonstrated such longevity. Of the five American cases marshalled by the Royal Commission on Capital Punishment in their discussion of the issue, only one makes reference to 'irresistibility' (*Commonwealth* v. *Rogers*).[27] The judge in *Parsons* v. *State*, the case which generated the modification to the insanity defence in the United States discussed on page 89, spoke only of the defendant's power to choose being impaired (*Parsons* v. *State* at 210, 211).[28] Irresistibility is an exacting standard: the military courts in the United States have interpreted it to require that the defendant would have acted in the same way had a policeman been standing beside him.[29] One Canadian judge doubted whether it should ever excuse.[30] Other legal authorities have argued that where an influence is so powerful as to be termed 'irresistible', the case for criminal sanctions against it becomes all the stronger (Baron Bramwell in *R.* v. *Haynes* at 898, 899).

Where the existence of an irresistible impulse is said to be at issue, however, usually what is being debated is the defendant's ability to control his behaviour (for instance in *Downs* v. *State* at 283, 284; see also Goldstein 1967, p.71). Doctors and lawyers have complained since the inception of the M'Naghten Rules that they fail to cater for the defendant who knows what he is doing and knows that it is wrong but is nevertheless pathologically driven to do it (see p.88). The persistence of the concept is not surprising.

The principal advantage of couching a test in terms of the actor's ability to control his behaviour rather than in terms of impulses is that this perceived weakness of the M'Naghten Rules – their emphasis on cognition at the expense of volition – is more fully addressed. The effect of mental disorder on volition is not restricted to the existence of abnormal impulses.[31] As the District of Columbia court put it in *Durham* v. *United States*, irresistible impulse, as originally conceived, 'gives no recognition to mental illness characterised by brooding and reflection and so relegates acts caused by such illness to the application of the inadequate right–wrong test' (*Durham* v. *United States* at 874).

The same point, using melancholia as an example of such a mental illness, was made by the Gowers Commission (Royal Commission on Capital Punishment 1953, p.110). As result of concerns such as these, the idea that an inability to control one's behaviour should be included in the insanity defence has gained considerable currency. In the United States, at the time of Goldstein's review, it was accepted in 18 states and in the federal system (Goldstein 1967, p.67). In England and Wales, in murder cases, it has been accepted that an inability to control one's behaviour can be grounds for a plea of diminished responsibility (*R.* v. *Byrne* at 404).[32] It has never been included in the insanity defence in England and Wales, however, and its use has been decreasing recently in the United States.[33] Why is this?

Several criticisms have been offered. The first is that a test of the ability to control one's behaviour is not necessary because all excusable cases are already covered by the M'Naghten Rules (see Hall 1956). By this argument, since the human personality is an integrated whole, any instance of impaired volition will necessarily affect the actor's knowledge of the nature and quality of his act. The difficulty with this line of reasoning is that it assumes that the courts use a broad definition of such knowledge when interpreting the M'Naghten Rules. As we have seen, they do not. A second criticism is that, while not all excusable acts are covered by the M'Naghten Rules, a control test would not improve matters. This is because a true test of responsibility would take into account people's unconscious motivation for acting as they do (see Weihofen 1954, p.85). It is not clear how this could be done. A third reason for the less-than-wholehearted acceptance of control tests, however, is a fear that the floodgates will open and that numerous responsible people will gain access to the insanity defence. In the nineteenth century one author described acts of so-called irresistible impulse as excessive indulgence (Renton 1886, pp.29–33). He would presumably have described the practice of excusing such acts in similar terms.

A further difficulty with control tests, however, is evidentiary. Although great play has been made of the difficulty of distinguishing acts which cannot be resisted from those which simply are not,[34] the distinction has never worried psychiatrists.[35] It has, however, worried lawyers, presumably because, if there is a difference, it is one which is extremely difficult to demonstrate in court. Whereas evidence from the examination of the subject's mental state can throw light directly on his beliefs, and hence on to his knowledge of the nature and quality of what he was doing, the link between abnormalities on examination and the defendant's volition when he acted is likely to be more tenuous. The best witness as to whether the defendant felt able to act other than as he did is the defendant himself.

THE PRODUCT TEST

The views of the nineteenth-century New England physician Isaac Ray, concerning the shortcomings of legal tests of insanity, were described on page 86. In the 1860s he entered into correspondence with Justice Doe of the New Hampshire Supreme Court. Doe was enquiring as to the cause of insanity, and was reassured by Ray as to its physical origins (see Reik 1953, pp.187, 188). Thus emboldened, Doe became, through his influence on the judgement in *State* v. *Pike*,[36] the author of what was to become the New Hampshire Rule. This judgement, passed down in 1869, was novel in at least two ways. First, the conditions under which the mentally disordered offender could be excused were stated with refreshing simplicity: 'If the homicide was offspring or product of mental disease in the defendant he was not guilty by reason of insanity' (*State* v. *Pike* at 585).[37] Second, the difficulties of defining mental disease and whether or not a particular act was its product were acknowledged by Doe. In his view, however, these were not difficulties which it was appropriate for case law to address:

> It is often difficult to ascertain whether an individual has a mental disease and whether an act was the product of that disease; but these difficulties arise from the nature of the facts to be investigated, and not from the law; they are practical difficulties to be solved by the jury, and not legal difficulties for the court. (*State* v. *Pike* at 581)

The views of Ray and Doe were received enthusiastically in England. Maudsley wrote that in future the 'product test' would be widely accepted and tests of knowledge would become historical anachronisms (Maudsley 1897, pp.113–119). In fact, the reverse occurred. Doe's initiative was never adopted in England. Outside New Hampshire, the courts in the United States have experimented only briefly with his suggestion. A century after Doe's judgement, a version of his test was introduced in the District of Columbia when the Court of Appeals in *Durham v. United States* held that an accused was not criminally responsible if his unlawful act was 'the product of a mental disease or defect' (*Durham v. United States* at 876). Within 20 years it had been abandoned.

The reasons were several. First, like the New Hampshire judgement described above, the Durham formula provided the jury with no explicit criteria to determine a defendant's responsibility (see Glueck 1963, p.96). Indeed, just as Doe had done, the court made a virtue of its failure to do so:

> The questions of fact under the test we now lay down are as capable of determination by the jury as, for example, the questions juries must determine upon a claim of total disability under a policy of insurance where the state of medical knowledge concerning the disease involved, and its effects, is obscure or in conflict. In such cases the jury is not required to depend on arbitrarily selected 'symptoms, phases or manifestations' of the disease as criteria for determining the ultimate questions of fact upon which the claim depends. Similarly, upon a claim of criminal irresponsibility, the jury will not be required to rely on such symptoms as criteria for determining the ultimate questions of fact upon which such a claim depends. Testimony as to such 'symptoms, phases or manifestations,' … will go to the jury upon the ultimate questions of fact which it alone can finally determine. (*Durham v. United States* at 875, 876)

This explanation, however, did not reassure the judges in subsequent appellate cases.[38]

Second, criticism surrounded the use of the word 'product'. Did this mean that the mental disease or defect was a necessary and sufficient condition for the defendant to have acted as he did, or merely that it was a necessary condition for his so doing? This was clarified when the court in *Carter v. United States* made clear that the requirement was not that the act be a direct or immediate result of the disease or defect, rather that, 'but for the disease the act would not have been committed' (*Carter v. United States* at 618). Necessary, then, not necessary and sufficient. The difficulty, as advocates of the Durham test have conceded, is that this places an extreme burden on the prosecution once evidence of mental disease or defect has been introduced by the defence. They somehow have to show that while the condition affected numerous aspects of the defendant's behaviour, it would not have affected that element which led to the criminal charge.[39]

Other criticisms have been that widespread adoption of the Durham Rule would lead to an unacceptable increase in the numbers of defendants acquitted on psychiatric grounds[40] and that the level of psychiatric provision, and particularly the level of secure psychiatric provision, is insufficient to cope with this increase (see Glueck 1963, pp.100, 101). Each of these points ignores what seems to be the fundamental question: what are the appropriate criteria on which to excuse? Once those criteria are in place, any increase change in the rates of acquittal will be defensible, as will the provision of appropriate levels of psychiatric provision. A more serious difficulty with the Durham formula is that by not identifying any other criteria it makes the absence of legal responsibility dependent solely upon the act being 'the product of mental disease or mental defect'. Since every voluntary act must be the product of some mental state or other, exculpation hinges on whether the defendant's mental state amounted to a 'mental disease or defect'.

This places a burden on the term 'mental disease or defect' which it is not equipped to carry. Implicit in the Durham decision was that legal insanity meant nothing more or less than medical insanity (see Moore 1984, p.229). This was made explicit in *Carter* v. *United States*, a case which post-dated *Durham* v. *United States* by three years:

> Many psychiatrists had come to understand that there was a 'legal insanity' different from any clinical mental illness. That of course was not true in a juridical sense. The law has no separate concept of a legally acceptable ailment which *per se* excuses the sufferer from criminal liability. The problems of the law in these cases are whether a person who has committed a specific criminal act...was suffering from a mental disease, that is, from a medically recognised illness of the mind.
> (*Carter* v. *United States* at 617)

The difficulty here is that the object of psychiatrists in labelling and categorising mental conditions is, if not always therapeutic,[41] certainly not exculpatory. Modern international classifications include many conditions which could not be regarded as excusing by either the character or choice theories of excuse. In the *International Classification of Diseases* (World Health Organisation 1992) these include nightmares, premature ejaculation and non-dependent vitamin abuse. In addition, the Classification includes numerous other conditions, such as the personality disorders, whose capacity to exculpate is, to say the least, controversial. Psychiatrists do not include such conditions because they wish to broaden the range of exculpation but because they wish to be able to describe, in a reliable fashion, the people who come to see them.[42] The *International Classification of Diseases* specifically avoids using the terms 'mental disease' and 'mental illness' and states in the introduction that even 'mental disorder' is an inexact description of its contents (World Health Organisation 1992, p.5).

For these reasons, product tests have failed to gain the widespread acceptance which Maudsley predicted. The arguments put forward by Judge Doe and his contemporaries[43] in nineteenth-century New Hampshire, however, are substantial. They are involved but hinge, I think, on three points. First, there is a common-law tradition of excusing the insane which pre-dates all of the tests of insanity which have been described here. Second, insanity is not defined by courts in the first instance. Any legal definition must derive from a more general meaning of the term. Third, and as a consequence of these first two, when the judges in M'Naghten's case (and their predecessors dating back to Tracy and beyond) established criteria for insanity, they were doing no more than describing what madness meant to them. If madness means something different some years later then the rules can change.[44] The correct interpretation of legal precedent is that an excuse stems not from the M'Naghten Rules (or any other set of criteria), but from insanity itself.[45]

AUTOMATISM

Aristotle thought that in order to be worthy of praise or blame an act had to be voluntary. An act which was not voluntary could attract only pardon or pity. There is a difficulty, however, in that translations of Aristotle suggest that he thought there were several kinds of involuntariness. In *Ethica Nicomachea* (1109b35) it is first stated that an involuntary act is one conducted in the context of compulsion or ignorance. Later in the same passage, however, it is suggested that those deeds where physical compulsion is absent but where we nevertheless feel obliged to behave in a certain way should be regarded as involuntary. Throwing one's goods overboard in a storm in order to save oneself and one's passengers is described as, 'voluntary, but in the abstract perhaps involuntary' (1110a18). A third definition uses as its criterion the extent to which the actor's motivation is internal: '...now the man acts voluntarily; for the principle that moves the instrumental parts of the body in such actions is in him, and the things of which the moving principle is in a man himself are in his power to do or not to do' (1110a15).

Not all of these definitions would be widely accepted today. The first allows ignorance to generate involuntariness: 'I did not know that you were standing behind the target and my action in shooting you should therefore be regarded as involuntary.' Ignorance is, in certain circumstances, a defence in Anglo-American law[46] but acts consequent upon such ignorance would not now be described as involuntary. Similarly with the second form of involuntariness described in the translations of Aristotle. Necessity can occasionally be a defence to a criminal charge (see the discussion of necessity as a defence in Chapter 2) but actions carried out by virtue of that necessity would not be described as involuntary. Closer to the modern definition of voluntariness is the third description in *Ethica Nicomachea*, that which relates to the extent to which the actor can truly be said to be generating the action. Defined in this way, involuntary acts almost always provide an excuse at law. The one exception to this rule is where the involuntary act occurred while the actor was in a state of self-induced intoxication (see *R*. v. *Lipman*; *R*. v. *Majewski*). This rule is usually held to stem from the perceived social danger of allowing those who commit crimes when very drunk to be found not guilty (see Smith and Hogan 1996, p.39).

Examples of involuntary acts provided in the literature include that of a case of wounding where the defendant, who was holding a knife, had his arm grabbed by someone else, who then propelled the knife into a third party (see Smith and Hogan 1996, pp.38, 39). Another example offered is where the defendant's fist flew out and struck someone as part of St Vitus' dance.[47] It is a criterion of voluntariness in Anglo-American law that the conduct be willed (see Duff 1990, pp.177–118; Smith and Hogan 1996, p.38 *et seq*). If it is not, then there is no *actus reus* because the actor did not 'do'[48] the act.[49] This definition of 'involuntary' has been held to include instances where the actor was subject to no physical duress. If a driver was attacked by a swarm of bees and lost control of his vehicle as a result, he would not legally be said to be 'driving' (*Hill* v. *Baxter*). This is important from the point of view of mental-state excuses. Some involuntary acts are the result of psychiatric and other medical conditions. These acts are called 'automatisms'.

A description of automatism was provided by Hart (1968):

> What is missing in these cases appears to most people as a vital link between mind and body; and both the ordinary man and the lawyer might well insist on this by saying that in these cases there is not 'really' a human action at all and certainly nothing for which someone should be made criminally responsible, however 'strict' legal responsibility might be. (p.107)

The definition which is most commonly quoted in England and Wales is that from *R*. v. *Bratty* (401): '…the state of a person who, though capable of action, is not conscious of what he is doing. It means unconscious involuntary action and is a defence because the mind does not go with what is being done.'[50] The judge was thus offering, in addition to the requirement that an act be involuntary, the further criterion that it be unconscious.

The use of two criteria, voluntariness and consciousness, offers, in theory, grounds for confusion. What of acts which are conscious but involuntary, or unconscious but voluntary? In practice, this has not been a problem. It is difficult to imagine an unconscious voluntary action. Conscious involuntary actions do exist: sneezing and shivering are examples. They are not goal directed, however, and are unlikely to lead to criminal behaviour. The situation would change if the courts accepted that defendants can have multiple personalities, and that the separate personalities can be aware of each other's activities (see the discussion of multiple personality in the previous chapter). This has not happened yet.

In the United States, the automatism defence is similarly available to defendants who acted in a state of unconsciousness or semi-consciousness, the rationale offered by legal authorities again being that defendants in such a state must have been acting involuntarily (LaFave and Scott 1972, p.337). The question arises: if the defence is based on the principle that someone should not be punished for an involuntary act, why should consciousness be introduced as a criterion at all?

The answer may stem from what Schopp (1991, p.20), in a different context, referred to as the 'evidentiary' role of certain symptoms and signs. Psychological involuntariness is not something which one can see. The best informed witness is the defendant himself. Since the courts can hardly rely on his evidence as to whether or not his action was involuntary, there is a need to identify other signs which indicate that this is the case. Consciousness is one such sign. The law regards an act as involuntary when that act is the result of a condition which reduces the defendant's level of consciousness. In England and Wales, the list of conditions includes cerebral tumours, arteriosclerosis, epilepsy, sleep-walking, diabetes, concussion and the administration of sedative drugs (see Smith and Hogan 1996, p.41). In the United States, a similar list of conditions which excuse by impairing consciousness has been described (Eichelberger 1984, p.1073).

Once an action has been declared 'automatic', however, the question remains as to what legal disposal should be available. In England and Wales, there are two possibilities: the defendant may be found 'not guilty' or 'not guilty by reason of insanity'. Until 1991 the issue was of considerable importance. Defendants found 'not guilty' walked free from court, whereas those found 'not guilty by reason of insanity' were bound to be detained in a psychiatric hospital until the Home Secretary decided otherwise. Numerous appellate cases defined the criteria by which so-called sane automatisms (those which led to an acquittal) and insane ones (which led to detention) were to be distinguished (the debate has been reviewed by several authors; see Fenwick 1990; Mackay 1995, pp.31–62).

In R. v. Charlson, Mr Justice Barry implied that the criterion should be the degree to which the defendant knew what he was doing (R. v. Charlson at 864). In a later case, Lord Denning demurred, arguing that the distinction correctly depended on the propensity of insane automatisms to recur and to be manifested in violence (R. v. Bratty at 412). The present position is that an insane automatism is an automatism caused by an internal factor and which has on one occasion at least manifested itself in violence (see Clarkson and Keating 1998, pp.376, 377; Richardson 1999, s.17.94; R. v. Burgess; R. v. Quick).

Acts carried out while the subject was asleep had until recently been regarded as sane automatisms, perhaps less through logic than as a result of the courts' reluctance to detain sleep-walkers in psychiatric hospitals. In 1991, however, the courts yielded to the logic of the earlier appellate cases and concluded that if internal origin and liability to recur were the criteria, sleep-walking was an insane automatism (*R.* v. *Burgess*). By then, it had been decided that automatic acts carried out while the defendant was hyperglycaemic as a result of diabetes (*R.* v. *Hennessy*) or in the post-ictal stage of an epileptic seizure (*R.* v. *Sullivan* at 172) were also to be regarded as insane.

One example of an external cause is that of a blow to the head causing concussion (see *R.* v. *Sullivan*). An automatic act consequent upon such an injury would still be regarded as a sane automatism warranting a simple acquittal. Sufferers from post-traumatic stress disorder may suffer episodes of dissociation during which they are unaware of what they are doing (see p.65). Post- traumatic stress disorder is by definition the consequence of an external event. Is the automatic act of a defendant in a dissociative state following a traumatic event a sane automatism? The answer seems to depend on whether the external event is out of the ordinary.

A Canadian student attacked a woman who had recently jilted him, hitting her on the head with a rock (*Rabey* v. *R.*). The court heard that he had acted unconsciously, in a dissociative state, and that this state was a consequence of his rejection. He was acquitted on the grounds of sane automatism. The prosecution appealed, arguing that the cause of his automatism was internal and that the automatism was therefore sane. The Ontario Court of Appeal agreed and ordered a new trial; the stress to which the defendant had been subjected was one of the 'ordinary stresses and disappointments of life' (*Rabey* v. *R.* at 7), stresses and disappointments to which most people can be subjected without entering a dissociative state. The true cause of the defendant's being in such a state, therefore, must have been his vulnerable personality. Because this was an internal factor, the student's automatism was insane. Where the cause of the dissociation is rape, on the other hand, the cause has been held to be external (*R.* v. *T.*).

One authority has described the practice of distinguishing sane from insane automatisms on the basis of internal or external causes as 'absurd' (see Clarkson and Keating 1998, p.377). Why, one might ask, should the automatic act of a sufferer from diabetes be judged insane when that act is the consequence of high blood sugar as a result of too little insulin (*R.* v. *Hennessy*), and sane when it is the consequence of low blood sugar as a result of too much insulin (*R.* v. *Quick*)? If the purpose of making the distinction is, as Lord Diplock suggested, to protect society against the recurrence of dangerous conduct (in *R.* v. *Sullivan* at 172; see also Lord Denning in *R.* v. *Bratty* at 412), however, the practice can be defended. High blood sugar is usually the consequence of diabetes and, if the diabetes is untreated, will persist. Low blood sugar is usually the consequence of incorrect treatment which, in principle at least, should be less likely to recur.

This justification notwithstanding, some authors argued that it was unsatisfactory to label sleep-walkers and diabetics insane and to subject them to a rigid, arguably draconian, disposal. The Criminal Procedure (Insanity and Unfitness to

Plead) Act 1991, however, removed the requirement, in cases of insane automatism, to make a hospital order with indefinite restrictions on discharge. Judges
now have a range of options. These include the granting of an absolute discharge
and the making of a hospital order without restrictions. This flexibility applies in
all cases except where the defendant is charged with murder, when the judge is
still required to make a hospital order with restrictions on discharge (see Gunn
and Taylor 1993, pp.45, 46). What has not been altered by the Act is the practice
of labelling insane any automatic act which has resulted in violence and is likely
to recur.

In addition, one procedural consequence of the distinction in England and
Wales between sane and insane automatisms remains. The burden of proof in a
criminal trial usually rests with the prosecution, but lies with the defendant where
the plea is one of 'not guilty by reason of insanity'.[51] Thus if the defendant wishes
to rely on a defence of automatism, and if he can persuade the court that the
automatism had an external cause, such as a blow to the head, it is then for the
prosecution to satisfy the jury, beyond reasonable doubt, that his actions were not
automatic. If, on the other hand, the purported automatism has an internal cause,
such as his epilepsy, then it is for the defendant to prove to the jury, on the balance
of probabilities, that, to use the words of Lord MacDermott, 'the mind did not go
with what was done'.

In the United States, the usual practice has similarly been to incorporate certain
forms of automatism into the insanity defence. The criterion for such inclusion has
usually been the likelihood of recurrence.[52] Some debate has surrounded the
jurisprudential status of automatism. The implication in the *Model Penal Code* is
that it operates by denying that the defendant could have possessed the necessary
mens rea for the crime (American Law Institute 1985, Sections 1.13, 2.01). As
noted above (see p.97), this is not the view taken by most English writers, who
have held that the voluntariness of the act is an aspect of the *actus reus*. Other
American authorities also dispute the Code's assumption, asserting that an
automatic actor commits no crime not because he lacks *mens rea* but because he has
not engaged in 'an act', this being defined in its turn as a 'voluntary bodily
movement' (LaFave and Scott 1972, p.338). Theoretically at least, the distinction
is of some importance. If automatism denies the *actus reus* then it is possible for the
automatic actor to be found not guilty of crimes of strict liability (see Chapter 1,
endnote 1). This is not the case if automatism denies the *mens rea*.

To what extent do the legal definitions of automatism described here correspond with those provided by the medical texts? In general, use of the term is very
similar. In one respect, there is a difference of emphasis. The dual criteria
employed in the law, of voluntariness on the one hand and conscious awareness
on the other, have already been mentioned. Consciousness, however, is not an
all-or-nothing phenomenon to psychiatrists (the varying degrees to which it may

be said to be present were discussed in the last chapter). Automatic behaviour in epilepsy, in particular, may be associated with altered, rather than absent, consciousness. The subject may still be able to converse with others and effectively address himself to practical problems (Penfield and Jasper 1954, p.497). One neuropsychiatrist, after discussing several definitions which do make reference to consciousness and which, in his view, suffer as a consequence, has suggested 'an involuntary piece of behaviour over which an individual has no control' (Fenwick 1990, p.272).

In view of the similarity of medical and legal definitions, it is not surprising that the conditions described in the medical texts as producing automatic behaviour are broadly those which have been highlighted in the legal cases mentioned earlier. Cerebral tumours, particularly those of the temporal lobe, may result in the sufferer carrying out complex motor tasks of which he is to have no recollection (Mayer-Gross, Slater and Roth 1960, p.464). Automatic behaviour is a well-recognised concomitant of epilepsy in non-forensic settings, especially when the epileptic focus lies in the temporal lobe (Penfield and Jasper 1954, p.521). Other conditions mentioned in the appellate cases, conditions such as diabetic hypoglycaemia, drug ingestion and, if condition it be, sleep, are similarly recognised by medical authorities as sources of automatic behaviour. They have been reviewed by Fenwick (1990).

Is the automatism defence necessary? It has been argued here that, contrary to the opinion of Mr Justice Barry in *R. v. Charlson* (at 864; see the discussion of legal criteria on p.98), the primary function of the distinction, in England and Wales, between sane and insane automatism has never been to free those who did not know what they were doing. Rather, it would seem that the distinction exists, as Lord Denning argued in his appellate judgement (*R. v. Bratty* at 412), to ensure the detention in hospital of those whose violent behaviour is likely to recur.[53] To this end, over the years, more and more types of automatic behaviour have been removed from the category of sane automatism and included within the remit of the insanity defence. The most recent examples are the consequences of epilepsy and sleep-walking. At the same time, the provisions in England and Wales for disposal have been changed and the requirement for hospitalisation removed.

Could not the insanity defence alone be adequate for the disposal of all defendants who act automatically? From the point of view of exculpation, the legal definition of automatism does not seem to cover anyone who would not, in any case, be excused under the M'Naghten Rules. Automatic actors, as a result of their impaired consciousness, are unaware of the nature and quality of what they are doing. If the definition of disease of the mind was widened, they could then be dealt with like anyone else who fulfilled the criteria in the M'Naghten Rules. It seems likely, however, that there will be a continuing desire for the complete acquittal of those defendants whose automatic behaviour is externally generated and not likely to recur. Examples include the results of concussion and involuntary intoxication.[54] If this is to happen, the distinction between sane and insane automatism will have to be maintained.[55]

INFANTICIDE

In nineteenth-century England, infanticide was relatively common. Between 1863 and 1887 there were approximately 150 cases a year of the killing of a child under the age of one year, and such children comprised 61 per cent of all homicide victims (see Rose 1986, p.8). Mothers suspected of the killings were charged with murder. It is unlikely that many were put to death, however. Juries looked for any suggestion that the baby had died from natural causes in order to avoid bringing in a verdict of guilty. When they were unable to find such a suggestion, they would usually recommend the mother to mercy (see Walker 1968, p.128).

Perhaps due to the frequency of child killing, and perhaps, also, as a consequence of the disquiet of judges who were required to pronounce the death sentence in the near-certain knowledge that it would be commuted, the late nineteenth century saw several, unsuccessful, attempts to change the law (see Walker 1968, pp.129–131). It was 1922 before legislation was passed which permitted a woman convicted of killing her newborn child to be sentenced as if she had been convicted of manslaughter.

The present legislation in England and Wales dates from 1938, and permits a conviction for infanticide, rather than murder, of a woman who kills her child in its first year where the 'balance of her mind was disturbed by reason of her not having fully recovered from the effects of childbirth or lactation'.[56] A wide range of sentencing options are available. Most women are placed on probation (see Gunn and Taylor 1993, p.50). In contrast to the situation which seems to have obtained in the last century, such cases are rare. Since 1975, convictions have been running at six or seven per year (Bluglass 1990, p.527).

As a mental-state excuse, the infanticide defence is unusual in two respects. First, it restricts the availability of the defence to those whose mental imbalance has certain, specific, origins; namely, the effects of childbirth or lactation. Given that the cause of many forms of mental illness are as yet unclear, this seems illogical. Strictly applied, the requirement should mean that where no psychiatrist brave (or foolish) enough can be found to testify to the cause of an illness which the textbooks describe as of 'uncertain aetiology', the defendant could be found guilty of murder. In practice, this does not occur,[57] perhaps because of the sympathy which such cases elicit and the perceived low risk of recurrence. Second, the doctrine of infanticide makes no demand that a link be established between the deed and the woman's mental condition (Walker 1968, p.135). This is in contrast to the situation as pertains to insanity and diminished responsibility.

SUMMARY

There has been consensus, at least since Aristotle, that it is inappropriate to hold responsible for the consequences of their actions people who act involuntarily. The exculpatory function of the automatism defence has provoked little disagreement. Debate has instead centred on the function of the defence with respect to the protection of the public. In this regard, there has been a move towards making more automatic actors, including sleep-walkers and diabetics, subject to detention in hospital. There has been a simultaneous move, however, to end the mandatory nature of such detention and to allow judicial discretion in disposal.

By way of contrast, much of the debate surrounding the insanity defence has concerned the criteria which should be allowed to excuse. The search for such criteria has seen a move away from general tests of capacity, such as Judge Tracy's 'Wild Beast Test' (see p.85), towards a more detailed assessment of the defendant's reasons for doing as he did. The M'Naghten Rules make reference to whether or not a defendant knew what he was doing and that it was wrong. The control tests preclude conviction unless it can be shown that he could have acted other than as he did. If mental disorder excuses in ways other than by denying knowledge or control, however, these defences are open to the charge that they allow the conviction of the excusable.

One solution to the problem is to excuse any defendant who suffers from a certain level of mental disturbance; this is the approach adopted in the law relating to infanticide and by the Butler Committee in their proposals for the reform of the insanity defence. Another is to exempt from punishment all those whose actions were the product of a mental disorder; this is the approach which has been adopted in some parts of the United States. It has been argued that the product test places an unsustainable burden on the definition of mental disorder. The next chapter will discuss some alternatives to the tests of insanity which have been described here.

NOTES

1.   Although it is not clear that intention was the criterion which Bracton preferred. Elsewhere in his writings, it appears that he was concerned that the excusably insane should not only lack intent but be completely deprived of the capacity for reasoned action (see Walker 1968, p.28).

2.   Hale died in 1676 but his unpublished writings appeared postumously as *Historia Placitorum Coronæ*. This quotation is from page 30 of the first volume of the 1736 edition.

3.   The distinction of which is at least as old as the Statute of the King's Prerogative which was drawn up between 1255 and 1290 (see Holdsworth 1956, p.473).

4.   'Now touching the trial of this incapacity...this is a matter of great difficultly, partly from the easiness of counterfeiting this disability...Yet the law of England hath afforded the best method of trial that is possible of this and all other matters of fact, namely by a jury' (Hale 1736, pp.32, 33).

5.   Arnold shot and wounded Lord Onslow while the latter was returning from a fox hunt; he was found guilty, sentenced to death and reprieved after his victim interceded on his behalf.

6.   Hadfield fired a pistol at George III as he entered the royal box at Drury Lane Theatre. He missed.

7.   The special verdict, representing a third possibility in addition to guilty and not guilty, dates back at least to Matthew Hale. In the seventeenth century, it was an obligatory finding in cases of self-defence and an optional one in instances where the offender was insane. As was the case with the passing of the Act in 1800, the object seems to have been to allow discretion in disposal (see Hale 1736, p.305).

8.   Bellingham killed the prime minister, Spencer Perceval, and was convicted and executed.

9.   'That the insane mind is not entirely deprived of this power of moral discernment, but on many subjects is perfectly rational, and displays the exercise of a sound and well-balanced mind, is one of those facts now so well established, that to question it would only display the height of ignorance and presumption' (Ray 1839, p.29).

10. This is a curious argument. It introduces a utilitarian consideration – the need to prevent those who commit violent crimes from roaming the streets – into a debate as to the correct criteria for criminal responsibility. The origin of such a line of reasoning was traced by Ray to the medieval theologian Duns Scotus. Ray summarily rejects its 'absurdity' (see Ray 1839, p.47). The Solicitor-General's argument would make more sense if the alternative to conviction was release. By the time of M'Naghten's trial, however, statutory provision for the detention of those found 'not guilty by reason of insanity' had existed for nearly half a century.

11. In the trial of Hadfield (see p.86).

12. It is not clear whether M'Naghten had ever seen Robert Peel. In any case, he appears to have taken Drummond to be the Tory leader.

13. M'Naghten's acquittal led The Times, in a tone of ponderous sarcasm, to demand that the government clarify 'for the benefit of simple folks what in future is to be considered insanity' (6 March 1843).

14. Fitzjames Stephen's suggestion met with a swift and critical response from the medical profession. Doctor Bucknill, writing in the British Medical Journal, criticised Stephen's language, suggesting as an improvement, 'No act is a crime if the person who does it is at the time incapable of not doing it by reason of idiocy, or of disease affecting his mind' (1884, p.502). This seems to exclude from the insanity defence every mental condition with the exception of automatism.

15. But only as a second choice. Their preferred option was the abolition of the M'Naghten Rules with the decision on whether or not the defendant was responsible to be made by the jury with no statutory guidance (see Royal Commission on Capital Punishment 1953, p.116).

16. Williams was writing in 1961. An examination of the use of the insanity defence in England and Wales in the 1970s and 1980s revealed no evidence that the first set of criteria have re-emerged (see Mackay 1990).

17. In 1983 the United States Supreme Court ruled that where the consequence of a successful insanity defence was automatic and indefinite commitment, the burden of proof should lie with the defendant (see Jones v. US). This, more than the Hinckley decision, may have generated the changes in the states concerned (see Callahan, Mayer and Steadman 1987).

18. This may not have affected the number of defendants who have been able to make use of the defence (see McGreevy et al. 1991).

19. 'If the accused was conscious that the act was one which he ought not to do.' (R. v. M'Naghten at 210). It has been argued that the judges also used 'wrong' to mean 'contrary to the law' (see Guttmacher and Weihofen 1952, p.405). This they did, but only in response to the first question they were asked, a question which concerned partial insanity.

20. People v. Skinner (at 697) and People v. Rittger (at 909) are examples of cases where the courts have used a definition of 'wrong' based on the defendant's perception of public morality. In Wade v. United States (at 71, 72), however, the court decided that the defendant was not responsible if he believed that he was morally justified in his conduct, this despite an appreciation on his part that the act was contrary to law and public morality (see also the United States Appeal Court's discussion of their judgement in Wade v. United States in United States v. Segna at 232).

21. In R. v. Codere, when the Court of Appeal advocated a moral interpretation, they argued that this could be inferred from the defendant's knowledge of the law. 'Once it is clear that the appellant

knew that the act was wrong in law, then he was doing an act which he was conscious he ought not to do' (*R. v. Codere* at 27) (see Walker 1968, p.113).

22. Notwithstanding the comments above, this is also the usual position in the United States. See *State v. Foster* at 972, where the test was that the defendant be incompetent to discern the nature and criminality of the act; *State v. Boan* at 168 (unable to know that his actions were contrary to Kansas law); and *State v. Andrews* at 747 (wrong means that which is prohibited by the law of the land). One jurisdiction where the judges' original, moral, meaning has prevailed is Australia (see Fisse 1990, p.457). There the question is, 'Could this man be said to know…whether his act was wrong if through a disease or defect or disorder of the mind he could not think rationally of the reasons which to ordinary people make that act right or wrong?' (*R. v. Porter* at 189).

23. The defendant set fire to his flat while he was in it (*R. v. Dickie* at 178). The Court of Appeal did not think that his belief that this was a safe thing to do demonstrated ignorance of the nature or quality of the act.

24. I think that McAuley is wrong to discuss the insanity defence solely in terms of *mens rea*, but his argument raises an awkward point. Where the definition of a crime requires intent, *mens rea* is usually held to include knowledge of the consequence of one's actions. If a defendant presents psychiatric evidence to show that he lacked such knowledge, and hence to deny *mens rea*, he is likely to be told that he is running an insanity defence (see *R. v. Clarke*). If he understands the physical nature of the act and that it is wrong, however, he cannot fall within the remit of the insanity defence and is therefore not liable to be detained. The law seems to be saying that if *mens rea* is lacking, he should then be acquitted. This point will be returned to in the final chapter.

25. See Scadding (1990) for a psychiatrist wrestling with the issue; Scott (1958) for a psychologist doing the same.

26. In *R. v. Kemp*, Devlin described the state of the brain as 'irrelevant' (at 127).

27. Although even here the court first made reference to 'irresistible and uncontrollable' (at 460) and later stuck to 'uncontrollable' (at 461). There are, however, other cases, not mentioned by the Commission, where the word 'irresistible' is used (see *Flowers v. State* at 192; Goldstein 1967, p.69, footnote 8).

28. In a complicated ruling, the judge allowed two tests of insanity. The first comprised a 'M'Naghten' knowledge test. The second excused the defendant whose ability to choose was impaired 'solely' as a result of mental disease.

29. In *United States v. Kunak*, the court stated that the defendant's plea of irresistible impulse could only be allowed if 'the act would have been committed even though a policeman had been at the accused's side at the time' (at 358).

30. The law, he argued, effectively said to a defendant, 'If you cannot resist an impulse in any other way, we will hang a rope in front of your eyes, and perhaps that will help' (*R. v. Creighton* at 350).

31. Although this view is not universal. Wertham (1949, p.13) argues that the concept of irresistible impulse can safely be applied only by restricting it to the behavioural consequences of one medical condition; namely, obsessive compulsive disorder. Some of the difficulties which attend linking a defence with a particular medical diagnosis are discussed on p.95 above.

32. The judgement referred to the 'inability to exercise will-power to control physical acts'.

33. The second limb of the test contained in the American Law Institute's *Model Penal Code* refers to the ability of the defendant to control his actions. This was reviewed by the American Psychiatric Association in the wake of the trial of John Hinckley. It was rejected (see Insanity Defense Work Group 1983).

34. This was the reason given by the Butler Committee (Committee on Mentally Abnormal Offenders 1975, pp.221, 222) when they recommended against the introduction of such a test. The difficulty is partly resolved by employing the wording of the American Law Institute's test (1985), which requires that the defendant's 'capacity' to conform his conduct to the requirements of the law be impaired. In this way, evidence can be introduced concerning the defendant's behaviour on other occasions.

35. See, for instance, Maudsley (1897), referring to the 'obvious difference between him who will not and him who cannot fulfil the claims of the law' (p.119).

36. The judge in *State* v. *Pike*, Chief Justice Perley, charged the jury in accordance with Doe's dissenting opinion in *Boardman* v. *Woodman* (see Reik 1953).

37. The judge was equally forthright when he went on to give his reasons: 'When a disease is the pro-pelling, uncontrollable power, the man is as innocent as the weapon' (also at 585).

38. 'Whatever may be said about the rule of *Commonwealth* v. *Rogers* [see p.87] and similar rules they at least have something that can be called a standard, albeit an imperfect one, to guide the triers of fact. The *Durham* rule leaves the triers with virtually none' (*Commonwealth* v. *Chester* at 920).

39. For a discussion of the what might be termed, 'But for the disease, it would not have happened' approach, see Sullivan (1996).

40. A concern frequently expressed in debates over the proper criteria for exculpation (see endnote 10 and p.93).

41. The authors of the most recent version of the *Diagnostic and Statistical Manual of Mental Disorders* (American Psychiatric Association 1994) have conceded that the needs of lawyers and insurance companies influenced its design (Frances *et al.* 1991, p.410).

42. The arbitrary consequences of allowing medical categories to exculpate was demonstrated when psychopathy, previously excluded from the list of conditions which would qualify under the *Durham* rule, was included again following a weekend meeting at the local psychiatric hospital, St Elizabeth's. At least one retrial resulted (see Moore 1984, p.229).

43. The opinion in *State* v. *Jones* was written by Judge Ladd.

44. Hence, I think, the frequent references in the judgements of Doe and Ladd to scientific progress and the growing recognition of the physical basis of mental disease. This was their evidence that insanity was now known to be something different from that recognised by the judges in M'Naghten's case.

45. A similar point was made by Fitzjames Stephen. Even in the post-M'Naghten era, he argued, judges were still at liberty to direct the jury as they saw fit if they considered that the defendant's circumstances were different from those of M'Naghten (see Stephen 1883, pp.154, 155). There is a tradition in jurisprudence of dividing rules into the regulative and the constitutive. Regulative rules describe what should be done; constitutive rules govern, among other things, the circum-stances in which a regulative rule will be called into operation. To use the example provided by Collett (1977), a regulative rule requires that gentlemen stand when a lady enters the room while a constitutive rule tells them what constitutes a lady. The distinction goes back at least to Kant (1781, pp.210–211). Doe's point was that the M'Naghten Rules were constitutive, not regulative. The regulative rule was that the insane should be excused. The M'Naghten Rules described one set of conditions under which this could happen. There were others (see also Raz 1975, p.108).

46. But only where the mistake means that the *mens rea* of the crime is absent; a mistake as to what the law permits is not in itself a defence to a criminal charge (see p.23).

47. St Vitus' dance fulfils the need for examples of medical conditions which lead to complex invol-untary movements. The eponym refers to rheumatic chorea, also known as Sydenham's chorea, a condition which has become almost unknown with the reduction in the prevalence of rheumatic fever. The movements are usually jerky or writhing. Violent acts are not usual.

48. Although this would be regarded as unsatisfactory by some philosophers. Davidson (1980), for instance, held that all we ever really 'do' is move our arms and legs about. The consequences are, to some extent at least, out of our control and cannot be assigned to us with the same certainty (p.59).

49. This is a contentious area, however (see the discussion on p.23).

50. Credit for the definition is usually given to Viscount Kilmuir, the author of the House of Lords' judgement. In fact, Kilmuir himself made clear that he was quoting the judge who heard Bratty's case in the Court of Criminal Appeal in Northern Ireland, Lord MacDermott.

51. Insanity is the only exception at common law to the rule which states that it is the duty of the prosecution to prove all aspects of the defendant's guilt (see *Woolmington* v. *DPP*).

52.   See LaFave and Scott 1972, p.337. In *People* v. *Higgins*, the defendant's epilepsy was held to render him liable to disposal under the provisions of the insanity defence. The issue is discussed in detail by Fox (1963).

53.   'It seems to me that any mental disorder which has manifested itself in violence and is prone to recur is a disease of the mind. At any rate, it is the sort of disease for which a person should be detained in hospital rather than being given an unqualified acquittal' (*R.* v. *Bratty* at 412).

54.   But probably not the same desire to acquit the involuntarily intoxicated when they retain the ability to act intentionally; see *R.* v. *Kingston*.

55.   Evidence of such a continuing desire includes cases where magistrates have acquitted people who have acted in a state of epileptic automatism (see Gunn and Taylor 1993, p.59) and an apparent willingness on the part of the Home Office in the United Kingdom for this to continue to happen (see White 1991).

56.   In contrast to the 1922 legislation, which referred only to a newly born, the 1938 Act prescribed a time limit of one year.

57.   In fact, medical witnesses are willing to allow as evidence of mental imbalance for the purposes of the Infanticide Act conditions which they would not regard as producing an abnormality of mind for the purposes of a plea of diminished responsibility. See d'Orban (1979, p.570).

CHAPTER 6

Drawbacks of the Present Provision

The theory of excuse was discussed in Chapter 2. Chapter 5 examined mechanisms, such as the insanity defence and the offence of infanticide, by which excuses which are the product of a defendant's mental state have been recognised by Anglo-American criminal law. This chapter will discuss the extent to which these mechanisms adequately reflect the excuses which some mentally disordered defendants have to offer.

THE ELEMENTS

Current legal mechanisms[1] catering for the mentally disordered and excusable defendant contain several elements. The same applies to the suggested alternatives. As an aid to considering the issues involved, I find it useful to distinguish two types of element. The first addresses whether or not the defendant was in some way or other afflicted. The M'Naghten Rules, for example, require that the defendant suffered from a disease of the mind (*R. v. M'Naghten* at 210). The American Law Institute test requires the presence of a mental disease or defect (American Law Institute 1962, p.66). The infanticide legislation asks of the defendant whether she suffered from a mental imbalance as a result of not having fully recovered from the effects of childbirth or lactation (see p.102 above). Because this element addresses whether or not the defendant suffered from something, I have called it the did-he-have-it? element.

The second type of element addresses not whether the defendant suffered from a certain affliction but what he was able to do. I have called it the could-he-do-it? element. It may seem odd to ask this question of a defendant whose very ability to 'do' something illegal has brought him to court. But the second type of element is concerned not with the ability to act, but with the defendant's ability to function in a way which the law, or those who propose changing the law, equate with responsibility.

The could-he-do-it? elements of the M'Naghten Rules, for instance, require the jury to address whether or not the defendant could appreciate the nature and quality of his act, and, if he could appreciate this, whether he could understand the wrongfulness of what he was doing. The could-he-do-it? element of the

American Law Institute test asks whether the defendant appreciated the wrong-fulness of what he was doing, and, if he did appreciate this, whether he could conform his behaviour to the law. Did-he-have-it? tests inquire after a defend-ant's status, while could-he-do-it? tests inquire after his function.

Not all elements of the various mental-state defences can be categorised in this way. The product test (see p.93), although no longer in widespread use on either side of the Atlantic, falls into neither category. And to which category does the automatism defence belong? Medically, automatism is a condition. It might therefore be assumed that the automatism defence is a did-he-have-it? test. In court, however, the presence of automatism has hinged on whether or not the defendant acted voluntarily (see pp.96 *et seq.*). A voluntary act has been taken to mean one which is under the defendant's conscious control (see *R. v. Bratty* at 409). This is a test of function. The jury is being asked whether or not the defendant was able to control what he was doing. Legally, automatism would seem to be a category only to the extent that the requirements of this test of function are fulfilled. For this reason, automatism is categorised here as a could-he-do-it? test.

The did-he-have-it? element

To the extent that the law inquires into the cause of an allegedly excusable condition, it usually does so in order to disqualify evidence which could otherwise lead to an acquittal.[2] It does not usually allow the cause of a defendant's excusable condition to act as evidence of that condition, and hence to contribute to a defence. Childhood seems to be an exception.[3] More often, the law follows Aristotle, who thought that it was the presence of ignorance or compulsion, not the source of that ignorance or compulsion, which provided an excuse (Aristotle, *Ethica Nicomachea*, IIIIa).

Fitzjames Stephen (1883) thought that the same principle should apply in cases of mental disorder: 'The different legal authorities upon the subject have been right in holding that the mere existence of madness ought not to be an excuse for crime, unless it produces in fact one or the other of certain conse-quences' (p.125). The widespread use of did-he-have-it? criteria to exculpate the mentally disordered runs counter to these views. The presence of a condition, be it 'mental disease', 'mental abnormality', 'mental imbalance', or 'mental defect', is being allowed as evidence that the defendant was either less responsible or not responsible at all.

In France, the *Code Penal* provides that sufferers from *démence* should be excused (Garcon 1901, Article 64). It is for the psychiatrists to decide what constitutes *démence*: 'The question of whether such mental illness exists is not one for the law but for psychiatry…the criminal law can only accept its conclusions.'[4] In a sense, therefore, one of the tasks of the court – that of deciding whether or not the defendant is responsible for his actions – is being handed over to the doctors. At the end of the last century the dissatisfaction of French magistrates with this state of affairs led to their not requesting a medical opinion in cases where they felt that it might lead to a guilty defendant being acquitted (see Oppenheimer 1909, p.117). As a consequence, a number of mentally ill defendants were found guilty without any psychiatric evidence being heard (see Pactet and Colin 1901, pp.85–90).[5]

To argue that a question is being asked of the wrong people, however, is not to argue that the wrong question is being asked. A proponent of the did-he-have-it? approach could argue that the disquiet of the French magistrates would have been avoided if the jury, not the doctor, had been asked to decide whether or not the defendant suffered from one of a series of medical conditions. It is not clear, however, that this would improve the situation.

The problem which all did-he-have-it? tests have to overcome is that the presence of a medical condition is not the same thing as the absence of responsibility. In Chapter 2 it was suggested that our practice of excusing is best explained by choice theory. Choice theory holds that we absolve people from responsibility for what would otherwise be criminal acts where we feel that they did not make a proper choice to act as they did. Medical categories are not defined by the presence or absence of choice.

This would not matter if in practice the conditions which psychiatrists identify and treat are those conditions which interfere with the sufferer's ability to choose. In many instances, however, this is not the case. The most recent version of the *International Classification of Diseases* (World Health Organisation 1992) includes among the 'mental and behavioural disorders': nightmares, premature ejaculation and non-dependent vitamin abuse (see the discussion on p.95). The capacity to excuse of other conditions which are included in the Classification, such as the personality disorders, has been the subject of extensive debate (see, for instance, Duff 1993).

Even where medicine does identify a condition which interferes with choice, the problems for the did-he-have-it? approach do not end. Schizophrenia causes a number of the symptoms and signs – identified and discussed in Chapter 4 – which interfere with the ability to choose. When doctors diagnose schizophrenia, however, they pay little attention to the issue of when the diagnosis should cease to apply. If someone suffers for six weeks from delusions and hallucinations characteristic of schizophrenia and then recovers, both of the widely used international classifications require that he or she still be diagnosed as suffering from the condition even if they remain well several years later (see American Psychiatric Association 1994; World Health Organisation 1992).[6] The issue does not affect treatment and receives scant attention in the medical literature. If the law is to employ medical categories as a basis for exculpation, however, a point at which illness can be said no longer to be present needs to be identified.

A final difficulty with the did-he-have-it? approach is that the same excuse does not serve the same actor in every situation. Someone who suffers from obsessive compulsive disorder finds it difficult to concentrate normally on the activities of daily living because of their preoccupation with checking and cleanliness. If someone dies as a result of their negligence in failing to maintain their car, we may be inclined to excuse or at least suggest that their mental state at the time be allowed to mitigate. If the same person commits an offence by careful planning and execution, however, we are not so inclined, presumably because we find it difficult to see how poor concentration and preoccupation with cleanliness could have contributed to the offence.

With these reservations, the advantage of a did-he-have-it? test is that it removes the need for psychiatrists and courts to establish whether the defendant, at the time he acted, either lacked *mens rea* or failed to fulfil a set of statutory criteria relating to his mental functioning.[7] The results of attempts to meet this need, it could be argued, will always be unsatisfactory. First, the details of a defendant's mental state at the time of the act may be difficult to discern. This act may precede the trial by many months, and only the defendant can know for certain what was in his mind. The prosecution may call into question the reliability of his evidence, and, in any case, many people charged with serious crimes claim not to remember what happened. Second, intent can be difficult to prove even when the mental state of the defendant is normal (Briscoe 1975).[8] When the person suffers from delusions or hallucinations, and particularly when formal thought disorder disrupts the normal flow of his thoughts and speech, the task becomes more onerous still. Finally, the experience of being examined on these points by a psychiatrist, and especially of being asked to give evidence in court, may be distressing to a mentally disordered defendant.

It should also be acknowledged that the drawbacks, described above, of the did-he-have-it? approach do not apply equally to all cases. Where the nature of the mental disorder is severe, our tendency to excuse for different reasons in different circumstances becomes less of an issue: whatever the criteria for responsibility, the defendant is unlikely to meet them. Similarly, when the defendant is very ill, this illness is likely to be recognised both by the courts and by doctors. The difficulties of the did-he-have-it? approach arise particularly when the defendant's mental disorder is less pronounced. This point will be returned to in the discussion of structural issues.

A third point to be made in support of the did-he-have-it? approach is that the drawbacks, described above, can be minimised if the mental condition which the defendant is required to have had is one which interferes with choice. Thus a did-he-have-it? test might not ask whether the defendant suffered from an illness such as schizophrenia or manic-depression, but whether the defendant displayed certain symptoms, such as a reduced level of consciousness or altered perception. Illnesses such as schizophrenia and manic-depression may go into complete remission and are thus compatible with a normal mental state; individual symptoms and signs are not.

These advantages notwithstanding, and with the exception of France, it is unusual for the did-he-have-it? element of a test of responsibility to carry on its own the burden of exculpation. The did-he-have-it? elements in the M'Naghten Rules and the American Law Institute test coexist with other criteria, which address whether, at the time he committed the act, the defendant was able to perform certain mental functions. They will be discussed in the next section.

The could-he-do-it? element

The effect of the M'Naghten Rules (*R*. v. *M'Naghten* at 210) is to ask of a defendant, 'Was he was able to appreciate the nature and quality of the act and to recognise that it was wrong?' The effect of the American Law Institute criteria (American Law Institute 1962, p.66) is to ask, 'Was he able to appreciate the wrongfulness of his conduct and control his actions?' These are the only could-he-do-it? tests which have been widely adopted in Anglo-American criminal law. They will be discussed first. One widely suggested alternative is to ask, 'Could the defendant think rationally about what he was doing?' This will be discussed second.

Cognition and volition

The M'Naghten Rules have been the subject of criticism since their inception. The thrust of this criticism has been that the requirement – that the defendant has been unaware of the nature and quality of what he was doing or of its wrongfulness – is a 'cognitive' one. It makes no allowance for the excusable nature of acts done by defendants whose intellect is unaffected but who have been rendered unable to control their behaviour in a normal way (see Royal Commission on Capital Punishment 1953, p.111; the distinction between cognition and volition is described on p.55 above).

Not everyone would agree that the M'Naghten Rules preclude the use of 'volitional' evidence to demonstrate that the accused was not responsible. Fitzjames Stephen thought that the M'Naghten Rules were broad enough to exculpate those who acted under the influence of an abnormal impulse:[9] 'The power of self control must mean a power to attend to distant motives and general principles of conduct and to connect them rationally with the particular act under consideration…a man who cannot control himself does not know the nature of his acts' (Stephen 1883, pp.170, 171). Stephen's argument would carry more weight today if right and wrong were required to be distinguished on moral grounds. In England and Wales, however, the distinction is now held to refer only to the legality, or otherwise, of the act (*R. v. Windle*, but see p.120, endnote 16). In these circumstances, the task of applying 'general principles of conduct' to the behaviour in which one is engaging becomes less exacting, and the potential for using the M'Naghten Rules to excuse those whose volition has been affected by disease less evident.

If an inability to control one's conduct is to be allowed to excuse, therefore, a new set of criteria have to be introduced. This has been attempted. When the test is referred to as one of 'irresistible impulse' it has been received less than sympathetically by the courts (see Chapter 5). Nevertheless, the case for excusing some of those whose mental disorder leaves them with no recourse to the M'Naghten Rules is a strong one. If a man suffering from manic-depressive illness tries to kill his family in the deluded belief that this is the best thing for them, his responsibility is reduced according to both the choice and character theories of excuse (see Chapter 2). His choice was impaired by his illness and his act did not reflect his character. He has no recourse to the M'Naghten Rules, because he knew what he was doing and that it was against the law, yet he deserves to be found not guilty of attempted murder.

Perhaps as a result, when tests of volition are couched not as 'irresistible impulse' but in their 'control' form, they have found more ready acceptance. The American Law Institute test refers, in its second limb, to the capacity to conform one's behaviour to the law (American Law Institute 1962, p.66), and the partial defence of diminished responsibility in England and Wales permits a defendant to be found not guilty if he is unable to exercise will-power to control his physical acts (*R. v. Byrne*). There is an ambivalence regarding the degree to which it is appropriate to exculpate on volitional grounds, however, an ambivalence evident in the failure to allow a 'control' element into the insanity defence in England and Wales (see the discussion by the Royal Commission on Capital Punishment, 1953, pp.93–96) and the American Psychiatric Association's recommendation that the second limb of the American Law Institute test be dropped (Insanity Defense Work Group 1983). It was suggested in the previous chapter that this ambivalence stems, in part, from evidentiary considerations: how can the court be sure that, on this occasion, the defendant could not have controlled his behaviour?

Rationality

Rationality is a test of sanity which finds much support among lawyers and philosophers (see Feinberg 1970; Fingarette and Fingarette Hasse 1979; McAuley 1993; Moore 1984; Radden 1985).[10] It has already appeared as a test of the culpability of the mentally disordered. In Scotland, Lord Strachan told the jury that for a finding of not guilty by reason of insanity there must be 'some alienation of the reason in regard to the act committed' (*HM Advocate v. Kidd* at 70). And a similar line was taken by the Second Division in a civil case in Scotland, where the issue was felt to be whether the action of the accused was 'influenced by his insanity, so that he was disabled from forming a rational decision in regard to [the act]' (*Breen* v. *Breen* at 185). This is now the test of insanity in Scots law (Gordon 1978, pp.374–376). Rationality also makes a brief appearance in the M'Naghten Rules. In order to be excused, the defendant is required to demonstrate a 'defect of reason' (*R.* v. *M'Naghten* at 210).

An aside of one proponent of reason as a test of responsibility is that such a test is incompatible with the 'medical model' of mental illness.[11] By this argument, claimed to derive from Foucault (1961, p.278), the sixteenth- and seventeenth-century notion of madness as a loss of reason (*deraison*) has come to be replaced, through the advances of medical science, by a medical model (*folie*). But are these two points of view incompatible? To the extent that madness was seen in the sixteenth and seventeenth centuries as demonstrating a lack of reason, it would be seen similarly today. Reason, or rather the lack of it, is part of the phenomenology of madness. What medicine claims to have demonstrated is that, in some instances at least, the origins of this lack of reason lie somewhere other than in the spirit world. Views of the causes of madness have changed, but irrationality is still an accepted part of the phenomenology.

It is difficult to define irrationality, however. The law of Scotland leaves to the jury the questions of what exactly irrationality is and how much of it will suffice to excuse. Is it possible to go further than this and define rationality in sufficient detail to allow the development of a could-he-do-it? test based on the actor's capacity to make rational decision in regard to the act in question? For this to happen, two things would seem to be necessary. The first is a definition of rationality. The second is a description of the way in which a lack of rationality reduces our responsibility for the things we do.

Some writers on rationality define it only in the most general terms.[12] Moore (1984) gives more details (pp.101–104). Rationality requires a person to act in response to a set of desires in a way which is logical or 'valid'. For this to be the case, several conditions have to be fulfilled. The desires must be 'intelligible as something a person could want'. Wanting to carry all of one's green books to the roof, for no further reason than having them on the roof, is an example of a desire which is unintelligible. This requirement for intelligibility, Moore concedes, is not much of a constraint on what will be deemed rational. The limits of our empathy can be quite broad, at least 'once we make the effort to be non-parochial in our understanding of others'. For this reason, he introduces further constraints. One is that, in order to contribute to rational acts, desires should be consistent both over time and one with another. They must be transitive; that is, capable of being ordered according to the priorities of the actor. Finally, they must be 'correct'.[13] To complement this analysis of desires, Moore offers a list of similar constraints which beliefs must obey if they are to contribute to rational acts (pp.104–106).

How, then, does a lack of rationality interfere with responsibility? To Dennett (1969) it does so through its effect on the capacity for intentional action. 'We exculpate the insane,' he writes, 'on the grounds that rationally directed verbal stimulation fails to have its proper effect' (p.177). Because they do not alter their actions in a rational way in response to our (hopefully) rational advice, they are to be excused. But it may be that, while insane people can behave irrationally, it is some feature of insanity other than their inadequate response to rational advice which leads us to excuse. Indeed, Dennett's own examples seem to suggest this. He points out that in referring to mad people we say such things as, 'There's no point arguing with him', or, 'He won't listen to reason.' When we say these things of a partner or colleague, we are seldom seeking to excuse.

For Moore, the question of how irrationality interferes with responsibility does not arise: the terms 'rational' and 'responsible' are synonymous. His analysis of rationality, described above, thus reflects his view of the circumstances in which mentally disordered offenders deserve to be excused. Feinberg (1970) shares Moore's willingness to equate rationality with responsibility but his analysis is somewhat different. Moore thinks that the motives of the mentally ill are irrational because they are unintelligible. Feinberg's view is that they are unintelligible because they are irrational (p.285). More importantly, Feinberg differs from Moore in his analysis of our reasons for regarding some people as irrational and therefore, in his eyes, less responsible.

Feinberg is concerned that intelligibility, one of Moore's criteria, depends in large part on the capacities of our imaginations. Instead of intelligibility, he argues, perhaps self-interest could be the test of a rational act. The problem with this, as Feinberg acknowledges, is that many people, so-called kleptomaniacs, for instance, can act out of self-interest (at least short-term self-interest) and still be considered irrational. And not all crimes by normal individuals are carried out for gain. Feinberg's way out of the cul-de-sac is to argue that the motives of the mentally disordered are not self-interested or unself-interested: they are just not interested at all (1970, p.286). Such motives are, in his term, 'senseless'; they are incoherent, in that they do not serve the actor's best interests, even in that actor's own terms, and the actor lacks insight into his or her motivation (p.288).

Could any of these analyses form the basis of a could-he-do-it? test of responsibility? The courts would have to decide what to do with people who claim to have acted 'for no particular reason'. Duff (1990) has pointed out that this statement does not usually deny that the actor did what he did for a reason, or indeed that the reason was a good one. Rather, it implies that the action was desirable or pleasurable in some obvious way and that no further explanation is required.[14] In offering such a description we may also be implying that, in our opinion, the action was trivial. One might dispute this alleged triviality, especially where the act was a violent one. But what would the advocates of rationality as a test of criminal responsibility do when a defendant claims to have acted 'for no particular reason'?

A second difficulty is that many of our actions are carried out not for one reason but for several. Thus one man might attack another because of a long-standing dislike and because it has recently come to his attention that his victim is having an affair with his wife. It is not clear what the advocates of rationality as a test would have a jury do if the long-standing dislike was rational but the belief concerning infidelity was a delusion. Which reason should be tested for adequacy?

A third problem relates to the heterogeneity of excuses. Insane actors can excuse themselves using one of several explanations of their behaviour, and in each of these explanations their 'irrationality' takes a different form. Some will claim that they were unable to control themselves in the normal way, some that their beliefs concerning the circumstances were mistaken. In other cases it will be impossible to say anything about their desires and beliefs at the time they acted. It seems unlikely that one aspect of cognitive function can be the litmus test of responsibility in all of these situations.[15]

Difficulties with the could-he-do-it? element

The review of did-he-have-it? tests concluded that the difficulties which attend those tests are less where the defendant's symptoms are severe (see p.111). The same applies to the could-he-do-it? approach. No controversy surrounds the exculpation of defendants whose mental disorder renders them unable to control their voluntary acts consciously. When the proper limits of the automatism defence have been debated in court, the argument has concerned whether or not the successful defendant should be made subject to the provisions of the insanity legislation, not whether he should be held responsible for what he has done (see p.91).

When it is used in less extreme cases, however, the could-he-do-it? approach can be criticised in two ways. First, it can be argued that some excusable defendants are not covered because the mental function being examined is not the correct one from the point of view of assessing responsibility. Thus the M'Naghten Rules are criticised for their omission of an explicit volitional element. Tests of rationality, depending on the definition of rationality employed, run the risk of failing to provide for defendants who reason normally in some respects but whose mental states preclude their being held responsible for the act in question.

Conversely, it can be argued that the could-he-do-it? element is over-inclusive. The M'Naghten Rules and the American Law Institute test both ask whether the defendant knew what he was doing was wrong. If he did not, and the other elements of the defence are fulfilled, he can be found not guilty. 'Wrong', in the M'Naghten Rules, is sometimes taken to mean 'morally wrong'.[16] Aristotle thought that ignorance of moral values was not necessarily an excuse[17] and this is the current position in England and Wales in respect of the insanity defence. Used on its own, and interpreted to mean 'morally wrong', this part of the M'Naghten Rules and the American Law Institute test would render a defence available to some defendants currently regarded as responsible.

The only way the could-he-do-it? element of a test of responsibility could avoid these criticisms is by addressing directly that aspect of a defendant's mental state which excuses him. The theory of excuses was discussed in Chapter 2. It was suggested there that the most satisfactory explanation of our practice of excusing certain actors in certain situations is provided by choice theory. It follows that a could-he-do-it? test should ask of a defendant, 'Could he make a proper choice to act as he did?' This provides somewhat more guidance to a jury, in terms of the meaning of responsibility, than does the doctrine of diminished responsibility in England and Wales. It provides substantially less than is contained in the M'Naghten Rules. If further guidance is required, one way in which it could be provided will be described in the next chapter.

STRUCTURAL ISSUES

Two elements have been identified in the legal mechanisms for the exculpation of the mentally disordered. Some shortcomings of each element have been discussed. The did-he-have-it? approach fails to address the heterogeneity of excuses. The could-he-do-it? approach can be criticised on the basis that the mental function being examined is the incorrect one for the purposes of exculpation. In practice, however, the insanity defence in Anglo-American criminal law has usually employed the two approaches simultaneously. The M'Naghten Rules and the American Law Institute test contain both did-he-have-it? and could-he-do-it? elements.

A number of proposed alternatives to current insanity defences have similarly contained two stages. Glueck (1963) suggested that the jury be told:

> If you are convinced that the defendant, at the time of the crime, was suffering from mental disease or defect which impaired his powers of thinking, feeling, willing or self-integration, and that such impairment probably made it impossible for him to understand or control the act he is charged with as the ordinary, normal person understands and controls his acts, you should find him 'Not guilty on the ground of insanity.' (p.105)

Glueck is requiring, first, a disease or defect causing psychological impairment and, second, a defect of understanding or control.

Schopp (1991) proposed that an actor should be found not guilty by reason of insanity if his conduct 'were the product of an action-plan selected through the exercise of substantially impaired cognitive processes that prevented the defendant from engaging in the ordinary process of practical inference from his wants and beliefs to an action-plan' (p.199). Schopp's test, like the M'Naghten Rules, is cognitive in emphasis.[18] It requires, first, cognitive impairment and, second, defective practical inference. It is also couched in technical language which would be difficult for a jury to understand and apply.

There are substantial differences between the two suggestions. That of Schopp consists of a requirement for substantially impaired intellectual ability (a could-he-do-it? test) with one that the act be the product of this impairment. Glueck prefers an expanded definition[19] of mental disease or defect (a did-he-have-it? test) combined with a requirement of defective understanding or control (a could-he-do-it? test). The difficulty for all multi-stage tests, however, is that each of their stages is likely to carry its own disadvantages, and these disadvantages may be cumulative. Schopp's suggestion would generate opposition to the cognitive emphasis of its could-he-do-it? component, and, separately, for its 'product' requirement.[20] Glueck would have to defend both the did-he-have-it? and could-he-do-it? approaches. Combining tests can lead to the worst of all worlds.

This is only true, however, when the elements are combined in such a way that a defendant can only escape conviction by fulfilling the requirements of all them. In electrical terms, the 'elements' are then 'wired in series'. A successful defence under the M'Naghten Rules, for instance, must go through three elements. First, the defendant must show that he had a defect of reason. Second, he must demonstrate that this was caused by a disease of the mind. And third, he must show either that he did not know the nature and quality of what he was doing or, if he did know this, that he did not know that it was wrong. One alternative to combining the elements in this way will be discussed in the next chapter.

SUMMARY

This chapter has examined some of the criticism which has been levelled at legal mechanisms for the exculpation of the mentally disordered. Two approaches to exculpation have been identified, and each of these approaches is reflected in the various versions of the insanity defence. The first I have described as the did-he-have-it? approach, and the second as the could-he-do-it? approach.

The did-he-have-it? approach requires the jury to establish whether or not the defendant, at the time he acted, suffered from a particular condition. This raises the question of how that condition should be defined. Psychiatric labels, it has been suggested here, are not up to the task. I have also argued that the did-he-have-it? approach fails to allow for our practice of excusing for different reasons at different times, although I think this raises few difficulties when the defendant's symptoms are severe.

The could-he-do-it? approach, on the other hand, can be criticised on the basis that the mental functions which it requires the jury to assess are not the correct ones from the point of view of assessing culpability. The problems of each approach – did-he-have-it? and could-he-do-it? – are emphasised by the structure of the insanity defence, which requires a defendant to address all of a series of elements before he can be found not guilty. The next chapter will suggest some alternatives.

NOTES

1. Not all are defences; a successful plea of diminished responsibility, for instance, does not lead to acquittal.

2. Intoxication cannot negate recklessness if the intoxication was voluntary, for instance (see Richardson 1999, s.17.105), and the defence of duress is not available to a defendant who was pressured into committing a crime if he chose to place himself in a situation where that was likely to happen (see p.35).

3. At least when the child is under ten; see the discussion in Chapter 3, endnote 14.

4. 'La question de savoir si cette alienation mentale existe n'est pas du domaine du droit; elle ne releve que de la psychiatrie... Le droit penal pratique ne peut qu'accepter ses conclusions' (Garcon 1901, Article 64, Paragraph 25).

5. In this century, French law has developed a further requirement that, for the defendant to be excused, there must be some link between the mental disorder and the illegal act (see Lloyd and Bénézech 1991).

6. Each provides a category for cases where the subject has experienced one episode but has since been in complete remission.

7. The usual approach in Anglo-American Law: see the next section.

8. Hart (1968) argued that the courts often abandon the attempt to discover whether a person charged with a crime intended to do it (p.175). They rely instead upon presumptions, such as that whereby a man intends the natural consequences of his action, and upon objective tests, such as whether an ordinary man, who behaved as the accused did, would have foreseen certain consequences. The Criminal Justice Act 1967 required the jury to be instructed that they should decide whether the defendant intended or foresaw a result by reference 'to all the evidence drawing such inferences from the evidence as appears proper' (at s.8). The effect was to enact what many had thought to be the law prior to the more extreme words of one Lord Chancellor, 'once the jury are satisfied that the accused [was unlawfully and voluntarily doing something to someone] it matters not what the accused contemplated as the probable result or whether he ever contemplated at all, provided he...was a man capable of forming an intent, not insane within the M'Naghten Rules and not suffering from diminished responsibility' (*DPP* v. *Smith* at 327).

9. Although he thought that the M'Naghten Rules could be interpreted more broadly, Stephen's preferred alternative was an insanity defence which incorporated a 'control' element (see Chapter 5).

10. This enthusiasm has not been shared by many psychiatrists or psychologists: 'We must therefore conclude that the insane patient is not irrational in the sense that his reasoning powers are in themselves different from those of normal men. It is true that certain of his mental processes have a non-rational origin, but it is equally true that the great bulk of opinions and beliefs held by a normal man arise in a similar way, and we cannot therefore on this account attribute a peculiar irrationality to the lunatic' (Hart 1912, p.138). Hart's observation, that the insane do not represent a class of irrational people, is only an argument against using rationality as a did-he-have-it? test of

insanity. It could still be used, as described here, as a could-he-do-it? test whereby the defendant would be excused if the act in question was of 'non-rational origin'.

11.   See Radden (1985) who implies (p.68) that many delusions are rational responses to hallucinatory experiences. Although some investigators have speculated along these lines, it is probably not the case. Delusions, particularly when they are of a persecutory nature and when the sufferer is older, frequently occur in the absence of hallucinations. And Buchanan *et al.* (1993) found that when people are asked why they believe in their delusions, it is unusual for them to offer, as evidence, hallucinations.

12.   And defend doing so: 'The concept of rationality is probably no more precise or definite than many another such basic concept essential in human intercourse' (Fingarette 1972, p.203; for general definitions of rationality see Fingarette and Fingarette Hasse 1979; Radden 1985).

13.   By which he means that the desire stems from 'a moral belief that is true'. See Moore (1984, p.104).

14.   Duff is attempting to find an adequate definition of intention and discussing the possibility that an agent's intentions in action are his reasons for action (Duff 1990, pp.50, 51).

15.   If the judges who laid down the M'Naghten Rules had thought that it could, the insanity defence would presumably require only a defect of reason from disease of the mind.

16.   This despite *R.* v. *Windle* (see page 109); see Mackay 1995, p.104). In the United States the word 'wrong' is usually presented to the jury without explanation (see Goldstein 1967, p.52) and a moral interpretation is sometimes used (see p.90 above). The Australian courts have argued that it was the moral meaning which the judges in M'Naghten's case had in mind (see *Stapleton* v. *R.*).

17.   'Every wicked man is ignorant of what he ought to do and what he ought to abstain from' (Aristotle *Ethica Nicomachea*, IIIa).

18.   And all the better for it, according to Schopp. He continues, 'Major mood disorder that does not include severe cognitive impairment should not exculpate under the [insanity] defense because this type of psychopathology does not prevent attribution of the act to the actor as a competent practical reasoner' (1991, p.210).

19.   Glueck's definition is expanded in the sense that the M'Naghten Rules and the American Law Institute test provide no definition at all.

20.   For a review of the criticism which the 'product' requirement has generated see Chapter 5.

CHAPTER 7

Alternatives to
the Present Provision

The previous chapter described some of the criticism which has been directed at the legal mechanisms for the exculpation of the mentally disordered. This chapter will discuss three alternatives. The first is to do away with the insanity defence. The excusable mentally disordered, if they were to escape conviction, would then rely on other parts of the criminal law. This is usually known as the 'abolitionist' position, and will be discussed in the first part of the chapter.

The second alternative would combine the elements of a defence for the mentally disordered in such a way that the problems described in the previous chapter are minimised. This was suggested by the Butler Committee in England and Wales in 1975. The third alternative involves the construction of a could-he-do-it? test which addresses more directly that aspect of a defendant's mental state which renders him a responsible agent. In Chapter 2 it was suggested that this is his ability properly to choose.

THE ABOLITIONIST POSITION

One solution to the difficulties which attend the development of mental-state defences is to adopt the suggestion of writers such as Norval Morris and do away with them (Morris 1982, pp.53 *et seq.*; for prior advocacy of this position see Goldstein and Katz 1963; Kenny 1978; Morris and Burt 1972). Mentally ill defendants would then avoid conviction when the prosecution failed to prove three things: *mens rea, actus reus*[1] and that the conditions of any general defence which the defendant set up were not fulfilled.[2] Chapter 5 described the adoption of Morris' suggestion in some parts of the United States (Montana, Utah and Idaho) in the wake of the successful use of the insanity defence by John Hinckley, President Reagan's assailant (see Mackay 1988). The motivation which lay behind this legislative change, however, was different from that of Morris. Changes in the law of the United States were driven by a widespread fear that Hinckley and other defendants were 'beating their rap' (see Callahan *et al.* 1987, p.54). Morris was concerned that the insanity defence confused the provinces of law and medicine[3] (1982, p.55) but anticipated little change in the number of defendants acquitted if his proposals were adopted (p.65).[4]

Before Morris' proposals can be discussed further, however, one difficulty has to be addressed. The meaning of the term *mens rea* has changed over the years. Nowadays, it usually means intention, recklessness or negligence (Smith and Hogan 1996, pp.56–93).[5] This is also the position in Scotland, where Gordon (1978) has described it as 'specific' *mens rea* (p.382).[6] But older usage required, in addition, that the defendant be, broadly speaking, a bad person. Gordon calls this 'general' *mens rea*. In 1800, Baron Hume argued that, for conviction, there should be evidence of 'a corrupt and malignant disposition, a heart contemptuous of order, and regardless of social duty'.[7] If the prosecution could not demonstrate this 'heart contemptuous of order', the defendant could be acquitted. The process of excusing is similar to that advocated by Baron Hume's uncle, the philosopher David Hume, who argued that an excuse precluded an inference from an act to the actor's character (Hume 1739, p.582; see also the discussion of the theory of excuses in Chapter 2). A court which requires a heart contemptuous of order, however, needs to enquire as to the defendant's motive.[8] This the courts no longer do, and Scottish law has adopted the 'specific' definition of *mens rea*.[9] The example which Gordon gives is that of the man who commits bigamy out of religious duty. According to the law, he is just as guilty as one who does so for any other reason.

The meaning of *mens rea* may have evolved similarly in Anglo-American law. Blackstone (1769) thought that a criminal act required a 'vicious will' (p.21), and Brett detects the same requirement, for the voluntary doing of an act which both the actor and the world at large view as morally reprehensible, in the work of other eighteenth-century jurists, Hale and Hawkins (Brett 1963, p.40; see Hale 1736, pp.14–15, 'wilful disobedience'; Hawkins 1771, p.1, 'will to commit an offence'). In Brett's view, the major development in English criminal law theory since Blackstone, apart from the analysis of the conditions of blameworthiness, has been the removal of this requirement, as a condition of condemnation and punishment, for moral guilt to be present (see Brett's p.69).

The abolitionist complaint

Abolitionists argue that the criteria for exculpation, outlined in the various insanity defences, are unnecessary. One of these criteria is that the defendant be in some way mentally abnormal. In nineteenth-century New Hampshire, however, Judge Doe objected to juries being told what was, and what was not, mental disease:

> If a jury were instructed that certain manifestations were symptoms or tests of consumption, cholera, congestion or poison, a verdict rendered in accordance with such instructions would be set aside, not because they were not correct, but because the question of their correctness was one of fact to be determined by the jury upon evidence. (*Boardman* v. *Woodman* at 148)

Doe believed that abnormal mental conditions could excuse but that it was inappropriate for the law to attempt to define these conditions. The same view has been expressed more recently by Morris (1982, p.56).

If the availability of the various mental-state defences hinges upon a defendant's symptoms meeting the criteria for a diagnostic category, then Doe and Morris have a powerful point. Some reasons were offered earlier (see pp.95, 110). When doctors define medical conditions, they do so as an aid to classification and in order to communicate information about the patients they see. They are not attempting to separate those who are responsible for their actions from those who are not. No legal classification of mental illness based upon a medical one can be guaranteed to distinguish those conditions which interfere with our ability to choose,[10] and hence offer the possibility of exculpation, from those which do not.

But do the various mental-state defences really try to define mental illness? It is not clear to what Morris is referring when he criticises attempts to do this. Is it to the requirements, in the M'Naghten Rules (*R*. v. *M'Naghten* at 210) and the American Law Institute test (American Law Institute 1962, p.66) respectively, for 'mental disease' and 'mental defect'? These requirements can hardly be regarded as definitions. It seems more likely that he has in mind knowing the 'nature and quality of the act' (*R*. v. *M'Naghten* at 210), and having the 'capacity to conform one's behaviour to the law' (American Law Institute 1962, p.66). But these are not definitions of mental illness either. It is more true to say that they are statements which govern the conditions under which a mental condition will be allowed to excuse. The abolitionist case is best seen as denying the necessity for such statements.[11]

Seen in this light, Morris' case is similar to that of other abolitionists. This asserts that there is no reason to excuse a mentally ill defendant, which is not also a reason to excuse a sane one. Goldstein and Katz (1963, p.859) ask: 'What objective of the criminal law suggests the need for an exception to the law's general application – an exception which would require taking into account the mental health of the offender?' Their answer is that no such objective exists. Mental disorder, Goldstein and Katz argue, should only excuse when it denies *mens rea* or *actus reus* or when it makes available a defence such as self-defence.

Drawbacks of the abolitionist position

The first difficulty with the abolitionist position relates to the definition of *mens rea*. In California, Morris points out, the abolition of the insanity defence created a large amount of case law concerning when, and how, mental illness could deny the *mens rea* of first-degree murder in that state; namely, malice aforethought (Morris 1982, p.66). Morris sees this as a manageable problem which could be avoided by defining *mens rea* clearly. Could it? One form of *mens rea* is intent, the definition of which is far from straightforward (Ashworth 1995a, pp.167–175;

Duff 1990, pp.44–47).[12] Recklessness has similarly exercised legal scholars (Smith and Hogan 1996, pp.64–72; see also Law Commission 1989, pp.193, 194). In these circumstances the task of assessing whether or not a particular form of mental disorder denies a particular form of *mens rea* is likely to be far from simple, a point acknowledged by some advocates of the abolitionist position in the United States (see Goldstein and Katz 1963, p.872).

A second difficulty encountered by the *mens rea* approach is that the law does not always require the presence of a particular state of mind for conviction. The principle whereby criminal liability is based on what a defendant believed he was doing or risking has been called the 'subjective' principle (Ashworth 1995a, pp.152–155). In many instances, however, the courts are concerned not with what was in a defendant's mind, but with what would have been in the mind of a reasonable person in the same circumstances. This has been called the 'objective' principle (Ashworth 1995a, p.152).

The mentally ill defendant in *R. v. Bell* drove at speed into several parked cars in the belief that they were agents of the devil. He was convicted of reckless driving. On appeal he argued that, as a result of his state of mind, he lacked the necessary *mens rea* for the offence. The Court of Appeal held that the reason for Bell's apparent recklessness was immaterial. Since Bell's case the offence of reckless driving has been replaced by that of dangerous driving. Dangerous driving, however, is also measured against an objective standard (Ashworth 1995a, p.298) and for some other offences recklessness is judged by the standards of a reasonably prudent person.[13] Negligence is also measured by objective criteria. The defendant's conduct is compared to that of an ordinary, reasonably careful, man or woman (see Clarkson and Keating 1998, p.184; Richardson 1999, s.17.43). When objective standards are used, the abolitionist approach provides no mechanism whereby a defendant whose mental disorder rendered his conduct reckless or negligent can avoid conviction.[14]

A third problem attending the abolition of the insanity defence concerns public protection, a consideration which was apparent in the discussion which followed M'Naghten's trial (see Walk 1977, p.117). In the United States, the judges in *United States v. Currens*, after criticising the M'Naghten criteria, were at pains to ensure that some form of provision be maintained for the detention of defendants who did the act but lacked *mens rea*. They reflected that 'the throwing of the mentally ill individual from the jail back into the community, untreated and uncured, presents a great and immediate danger' (at 767). In England and Wales, if the arguments of the defence fulfil the criteria for a plea of insanity, the court can require that such a plea be made (*R. v. Clarke*). A successful defence then allows the detention of the accused, although since 1991 this has not been automatic (see Gunn and Taylor 1993, pp.45, 46). Although these public-interest considerations do not require an insanity defence, they would require the introduction of provision to assess defendants for detention under civil procedures were the insanity defence abolished (see Goldstein and Katz 1963, pp.870, 871).[15]

A fourth weakness of the abolitionist position relates to the change in the meaning of *mens rea* described earlier (on p.122). The usual requirement in England and Wales is that where the *mens rea* of a crime is intent it should have been the actor's purpose to achieve the result.[16] If the law was changed to reflect the abolitionist position, and if the definition of intent remained the same, Daniel M'Naghten would be found guilty of murder. Yet intuition tells us that someone as ill as M'Naghten should not be convicted. This intuition, it was suggested in Chapter 2, stems from our recognition that the choice which M'Naghten made – to kill the man he believed to be Robert Peel – was a defective one. A defective choice can be made in ignorance[17] or under compulsion. We are inclined to excuse, for instance, when we have reason to doubt that the actor knew what he was doing was wrong or when we suspect that he was unable to conform his behaviour to the law. Given the current meaning of intent, the abolitionist approach cannot make allowance for our desire to excuse in these circumstances. However inadequate M'Naghten's choice, it was still his purpose to do as he did.

Older definitions of *mens rea* offered more scope for the abolitionist position to protect from punishment those whose choices are defective. M'Naghten may have possessed the *mens rea* for murder when that *mens rea* is given its recent, 'specific', meaning. What he did not possess – or, at least, what there is more reason to doubt that he possessed – was the 'corrupt and evil intention', or the 'heart contemptuous of order, and regardless of social duty', described by Baron Hume (1800, pp.21, 22) and required by earlier, 'general', definitions of *mens rea* (see the discussion on p.122). A mental-state defence, if it is to excuse defendants such as M'Naghten, has to address not just the intent, but the way in which that intent has been generated.

No provision for excusing the mentally ill which relies on *mens rea* in its recent, 'specific', guise can do this. The question which the abolitionists ask was described earlier (see p.123): what reason is there to make special provision for excusing the insane? The answer is that special provision is necessary because the criminal law makes certain presumptions regarding the sane defendant. It presumes, for instance, that he knows what he is doing, knows the law and is free of internal compulsion. These presumptions are unsafe in the case of the mentally disordered. The circumstances under which they might be unsafe were described in Chapter 4.

THE BUTLER COMMITTEE PROPOSALS

This chapter has argued that if the law is not to convict some mentally disordered defendants when they have an excuse, a special test of responsibility is required. The previous chapter argued that those tests which have been introduced have attracted substantial criticism. The previous chapter also argued, however, that some of this criticism results from the requirement, present in many mechanisms for exculpation, that a defendant pass several tests simultaneously. A successful insanity defence, for instance, requires a mental disease, a defect of reason and a failure to appreciate the nature and quality or wrongness of the act. One approach which addresses this problem was suggested by the Butler Committee in England and Wales (1975, pp.222–230).

The Committee's proposals identify two situations in which a defendant could be found 'not guilty on evidence of mental disorder'.[18] First, if the defendant did the act but *mens rea* could not be proved, the new verdict would be returned if the defendant was found, on the balance of probabilities, to suffer from mental illness, psychopathic disorder, mental subnormality or severe mental subnormality. Second, if the defendant did the act and *mens rea* could be proved, then the new verdict would only be returned if, on the balance of probabilities, there was evidence of severe mental illness or severe subnormality.

The problem which attends, in electrical terms, the wiring of elements 'in series' is removed (see p.118). Defendants do not need to address all of the elements of the new defence simultaneously. Instead, the elements are wired 'in parallel'. Two different routes are available to a defendant who wishes to avoid punishment by showing that his mental state at the time of the act precludes his being held responsible. But is it right that different criteria would be allowed to operate according to which limb of the defence a defendant chose his defence to address?

It could be argued that, since we excuse people for different reasons in different circumstances (see p.116), the inclusion of provisions for exculpation which can vary according to those circumstances is an advantage. We excuse when someone's ability to choose is impaired. If someone can be shown to have *mens rea* because they acted with intent, there is at least some reason to suppose that they were choosing adequately and hence have no excuse. Intending, after all, involves many of the same procedures – such as being aware of one's surroundings and the consequences of one's actions – as choosing.[19] In such cases, where a *prima facie* case has been made that the defendant was responsible, it seems reasonable to demand evidence of substantial incapacity before concluding that he was not.

In cases where *mens rea* has already been denied by the subject's mental state, however, the task of exculpation is already accomplished. The role of the defendant's mental disorder might be described as one of making his excuse credible.[20] The Butler Committee were criticised for recommending the use, in these circumstances, of a definition of mental disorder contained in the Mental Health Act 1959. That definition, the Law Commission (1989) pointed out, included 'any other disorder of mind' (p.224) and they argued that it was too broad to be useful. It had the merit, however, of being the medical criterion used for civil detention. Those found by reason of mental disorder to lack the *mens rea* necessary for conviction would thus be detained only if they met the medical criteria for the detention of those who had not appeared in court.

By adopting the 'parallel' approach, it could be argued, the Butler Committee obtained the best of both worlds. The first, *mens rea*, limb deals with those cases which lack the required mental element for the crime in a way which avoids the drawbacks of the did-he-have-it? (see pp.109 *et seq.*) and could-he-do-it? (see pp.112 *et seq.*) approaches. This is tantamount to adopting the abolitionist approach to the exculpation of the mentally disordered. One difficulty with this approach, it was argued earlier (see p.125), is that some mentally disordered offenders do have intent despite their not having chosen in a normal way to act as they did.

The Butler Committee's proposals, however, allow these mentally disordered defendants who act intentionally to avoid conviction. They could do so by using the 'severe mental illness' limb of the defence. This is a did-he-have-it? test. As has been noted, such tests have found little favour outside France. By making the test a stringent one,[21] however, the Committee avoided most of the criticisms outlined earlier (see pp.109 *et seq.*). It is difficult to imagine anyone who fulfilled the criteria outlined by the Butler Committee being regarded as responsible for their actions. One advantage of using a did-he-have-it? rather than a could-he- do-it? test to cater for these mentally disordered offenders with intent is that the necessity of picking apart psychotic motivation is avoided.[22]

THE NATURE OF WANTING

The previous chapter argued that the various could-he-do-it? elements which have emerged have several disadvantages. By describing one aspect of adequate choosing, they allow the possibilities that some defendants who ought to be excused will be convicted and that some who ought to be convicted will be acquitted or found not guilty by reason of insanity. The previous chapter also argued that a could-he-do-it? test could best avoid these criticisms by addressing that element of a defendant's mental state which renders him responsible. That element is his ability to choose.

This section will describe a way in which this might be done. The argument derives from the work of Frankfurt (1971). Frankfurt's aim was to identify those features of ourselves which make us 'people', but his work offers a way of looking at notions of responsibility. It suggests a test – of the could-he-do-it? variety – whereby a defendant's responsibility for a crime would be held to depend on his ability to order his desires and beliefs correctly.

The essence of Frankfurt's differentiation between people and other creatures is the ability of people to form 'second-order volitions'. Someone may simultaneously want to play basketball and to watch television. In other (basketball-playing and television-watching) creatures, Frankfurt argues, the resulting action would be a simple product of the relative strengths of the two desires. The distinguishing feature of people is their ability to have another, second-order, want, one which cannot translate directly into action but which can influence the choice between more primitive, first-order, options.[23] Someone who is concerned to remain physically fit is more likely to allow her desire to play basketball to form her will than is someone who regards physical fitness as a form of vanity. For those who lack such second-order volitions and who merely rationalise first-order desires before acting, Frankfurt reserves the term 'wantons'.

The distinguishing feature of second-order volitions is that they involve a degree of self-monitoring (Frankfurt 1987). We are able to take account of what we are doing and modify our behaviour accordingly. It follows that there are two possible sources of internal conflict. A first-order desire, to smoke, for instance, may be opposed by a higher-order volition not to die from smoking-related disease. And second-order volitions may not always be in harmony with each other. One may wish to preserve one's health and to impress the assembled company with one's taste for Russian cigarettes. One's behaviour is thus governed by a series of layers of volition with competition possible not only between but within each level. Frankfurt's point is not that these conflicts need be resolved in any particular way, simply that their existence is one of the things which makes us human.

In a similar sense, although Frankfurt does not do so, it seems reasonable to talk of first- and second-order beliefs.[24] The desire to smoke is presumably associated with a belief that smoking is pleasurable. The concern not to die from smoking-related illness is presumably associated with a set of beliefs concerning the health risks. Free Presbyterians, presumably, have similar first-order beliefs and desires to anybody else but many behave very differently. Seen in this way, actions spring not from a few, easily identifiable, beliefs and desires but from a network, many of the components of which are incapable, independently, of influencing action.

The literature which describes actions consequent upon delusions includes the case of a woman who pointed a loaded gun at two meter-readers in the belief that one of them was a homosexual who had been impersonating her by wearing a mask since he was eight (Romanik and Snow 1984). No explanation of her behaviour based solely on her beliefs seems adequate. If she was so concerned about the meter-reader's mimicry, why had she not done something about it before he came to her door? Why did she think that pointing a gun at him would help?

The explanations provided by deluded people for their own actions are often strikingly inadequate in this way (see the examples on p.75). One author has even argued that the essential feature of a delusion is not its wrongness or the conviction with which it is held, but the fact that as a reason for action it is 'defective' (Fulford 1989, pp.215–218). Actions such as those of the woman who threatened the meter-readers, if they can be explained, require an explanation which invokes not just one abnormal belief but the simultaneous distortion of other aspects of the network of desires and beliefs which influence how we behave.

One of the difficulties with the choice theory of excuse is that it requires a description of what is to be regarded as a 'proper' or 'adequate' choice for the purposes of holding someone responsible (see pp.35, 117). Frankfurt's analysis suggests one such description. Although it is no part of his thesis, a proper or adequate choice might be defined as a choice consequent upon a proper or adequate ordering of one's desires and beliefs. When a defendant, at the time of the act, was unable to order his desires and beliefs adequately, it seems reasonable to regard his responsibility for that act as less than would otherwise be the case.

A could-he-do-it? test based on Frankfurt's analysis would ask the jury two questions. First, were the desires and beliefs which led to the defendant's act abnormal? Second, if they were normal, was the defendant able to order those desires and beliefs in a normal way? If the ordering of those desires and beliefs were distorted by one or more of the phenomena described in Chapter 4,[25] the defendant would be excused.

This approach might overcome many of the difficulties attaching to other could-he-do-it? tests (see pp.112 et seq.). It would avoid the criticism, to which M'Naghten Rules have been subjected, that no allowance is made for excusable defendants whose intact cognitive function nevertheless allows them to appreciate the nature and quality of what they are doing and that it is wrong. It avoids the problems of definition which attend the use of rationality as a test of responsibility. In addition, it avoids the problem of all did-he-have-it? tests, that of reliably identifying, at law, a class of excusable people.

Three problems arise, however. The first is quantitative. Any test of responsibility designed along these lines would have to include a term such as 'substantially': the court could not be expected to excuse if the distortion to the normal patterns of desires and beliefs was trivial. Such a term is open to several interpretations. This problem, however, is one shared by all could-he-do-it? tests. The American Law Institute (1962) wording makes reference to a defendant's 'substantial capacity either to appreciate the criminality [wrongfulness] of his conduct or to conform his conduct to the requirements of the law' (p.66).

A more serious problem is that of establishing which of a series of competing beliefs and desires succeeded in forming the defendant's will.[26] This difficulty goes to the root of Frankfurt's initial formulation. How do the numerous desires of different orders translate into action? Frankfurt's first answer was that we identify with certain first-order desires 'decisively' (1971, p.16); at such a moment, one's commitment 'resounds' (p.16) through the potentially endless array of higher-order volitions and action is taken. Frankfurt himself pointed to the difficulty of defining these terms.

He was later to argue that some decisions are 'wholehearted' (1987, p.44) because conflicting second-order beliefs are resolved before one acts. Not all actions are wholehearted, however, and Frankfurt concedes that the subject himself may be unaware of the degree to which second-order desires are resolved before action is taken. A jury asked to apply a could-he-do-it? test based on Frankfurt's formulation might have to assess the defendant's general ordering of desires and beliefs rather than his ordering of them in regard to the act in question.

A third problem is that such a test would make substantial intellectual demands on the jury. Whether or not these demands are excessive could be examined by presenting various drafts of the test to mock juries in carefully designed cases. This methodology has been employed to compare different versions of the insanity defence in the United States (see Simon 1967).

SUMMARY: THE PREFERRED ALTERNATIVES

An excuse is present where the actor's choice was impaired. The circumstances which impair choice, however, are generic only in the sense that they all produce excuses. The defendant may be affected by an inner sense that something needs to be done, a misunderstanding as to the circumstances in which he finds oneself or of the likely effects of what he is doing, or an inability to think clearly about the various options. Some of these are excuses for sane defendants.[27] Others are not.[28]

As a result of this heterogeneity, it has been argued here, the proposals of the Butler Committee have particular appeal. The *mens rea* limb excludes from punishment those mentally ill defendants whose excuse would also exculpate the mentally well. The severe mental illness limb does the same for those whose excuse, for various reasons (described in Chapter 4), applies uniquely to the mentally disordered. This second limb is, however, a did-he-have-it? test. Such tests have drawbacks. In particular, they do not address directly the defendant's ability to choose.

An alternative approach is to identify a defining defect in the mental function of all excusable mentally ill defendants. This approach is reflected in the M'Naghten Rules and the American Law Institute criteria. Both can be criticised for identifying on the wrong aspects of mental function from the point of view of assessing responsibility. The criticisms arise in part because we excuse for different reasons at different times.

If a could-he-do-it? test is to overcome these problems, it needs to address directly whatever it is that renders inadequate the choices made by some mentally disordered defendants. It could do this in two ways, depending on the degree of guidance which it was felt should be provided to the jury. First, it could ask the question on p.117, 'Could the defendant make a proper choice to act as he did?', leaving the jury to assign these words their ordinary meaning.[29]

If it was felt that this gave the jury insufficient guidance or too much discretion, the law could include a description of adequate choice with which they could compare the defendant's function. The jury would be asked to decide, first, were the defendant's desires and beliefs normal at the time he acted? If they thought that they were, they would be asked to decide whether the defendant was able to order those desires and beliefs in a normal way. If the answer to either question was in the negative, he would not be convicted.

NOTES

1. A crime usually requires the coincidence of an *actus reus* and *mens rea*. *Actus reus* refers to a voluntary action and *mens rea* to the mental state which accompanies that action. A few mentally disordered defendants can avoid conviction by claiming that they acted involuntarily and that there was, therefore, no *actus reus*. The majority, however, can make no such claim and in the absence of an insanity defence their defence would rest on a denial of *mens rea*.

2. Denials of *mens rea* or *actus reus* are not, technically, defences (see p.23). Rather, they avoid the need for a defence because the elements of the offence have not been fulfilled. The distinction is important with respect to the burden of proof (see p.100).

3. He went on to argue that it produced 'a morally unstisfactory classification on the continuum between guilt and innocence' (p.64).

4. Most of the requirements of the M'Naghten Rules, such as knowing what one is doing, are, in any case, requirements of *mens rea*. The exception is ignorance of what the law allows, an excuse for the mentally diseased under the M'Naghten Rules, which would not excuse a sane defendant (see Williams 1983, pp.642–646).

5. Not all definitions of *mens rea* include negligence, however (for one which does not, see Ashworth 1995a, p.93).

6. Gordon's use of the term 'specific' in this respect is not the same as that whereby 'specific' intent is distinguished from 'basic' intent in English law.

7. The definition of *mens rea* which Baron Hume is describing is based on that of 'dole', the mental element traditionally required for conviction in Scotland. Dole was described by Baron Hume as 'that corrupt and evil intention, which is essential (so the light of nature teaches, and so all authorities have said) to the guilt of any crime' (1800, pp.21, 22).

8. Motive is described by Gordon as the 'clue' linking character to crime (see Gordon 1978, p.215).

9. Although one relatively recent Scottish judgement stated that guilt requires proof not only of intention to do something but also that this intention be 'wicked and felonious' (see *Cawthorne* v. *HM Advocate* at 36).

10. The ways in which psychiatric conditions do this, by affecting processes such as cognition, volition and perception, were discussed in Chapter 4.

11. Morris argues, for instance, that to excuse someone because the M'Naghten criteria are fulfilled is to confuse 'the evidence for a proposition with the proposition itself' (1982, p.55). The proposition, to Morris, is that defendant is excusably insane. That he is ignorant of the nature and quality of his act is merely evidence in support of that proposition. More convincing evidence, for Morris, would be that he lacked *mens rea*.

12. The definition was discussed, with the recommendation that it be changed, by the Law Commission in England and Wales (see Law Commission 1989, p.193). The definition as it applies in murder cases was discussed by the House of Lords in *R. v. Woollin*.

13. The law of England and Wales has developed two definitions of recklessness, definitions ˙ are usually referred to by the leading cases. 'Cunningham' recklessness (see *R. v. Cur*

requires proof that the defendant was aware of an unreasonable risk. It applies to most offences against the person. 'Caldwell/Lawrence' recklessness (see *R. v. Caldwell* and *R. v. Lawrence*) requires proof that the defendant was either aware of an unreasonable risk or, in the presence of an obvious risk, failed to give the risk any thought. It applies to cases of criminal damage. The Caldwell/Lawrence test thus contains an 'objective' component. There is no requirement that the defendant recognised the risk, provided that the risk was obvious. The Cunningham test has no such objective component. Bell was convicted using the Caldwell/Lawrence test (see also Smith and Hogan 1996, pp.64–72).

14. For an example of objective standards in operation in England and Wales, and of the consequences for some mentally disordered defendants, see the case of *Elliot v. C.* discussed on p.20, endnote 9.

15. This practice is already followed in some parts of the United States (see Callahan *et al.* 1987).

16. This criterion has been widened on occasion to include instances where the forbidden act was not the defendant's purpose, but where he knew it was the near-certain consequence of what he was doing (see *R. v. Nedrick*; Richardson 1999, ss.17.34–17.41; Smith and Hogan 1996, pp.57–63).

17. This ignorance might occur normally, when we are mistaken as to the circumstances, or may be the result of an abnormal mental state; for example, when a sufferer from Capgras syndrome believes that a family member is really an alien imposter (see p.75).

18. The Committee preferred this phrase to 'not guilty by reason of insanity'.

19. Dennett (1969, p.117) has argued that one is responsible for an act when one committed it with awareness and rational control (see p.115 above).

20. A non-disordered defendant who claimed that he attacked someone in the belief that he was doing something else would not usually be believed.

21. The criteria required that the subject exhibit intellectual impairment, lasting and pevasive mood change, delusions, abnormal perception or thinking so disordered as to prevent a reasonable appraisal of his situation (see Butler Committee1975, p.229 and Appendix 10).

22. A potentially difficult and distressing task (see pp.69 and 111).

23. 'Someone has a desire of the second order either when he wants simply to have a certain desire or when he wants a certain desire to be his will' (Frankfurt 1971, p.10).

24. The concept of second-order beliefs which involve an element of self-monitoring has, however, been developed by Colin McGinn (1979).

25. Phenomena which cause abnormalities of consciousness, emotion, perception, thinking or attention.

26. This point, made initially by Frankfurt himself, was developed by Watson (1975).

27. A mistake as to the circumstances which denies *mens rea* permits acquittal with no requirement that the defendant be mentally disordered.

28. Ignorance of what the law allows is not a defence for a sane defendant.

29. As they are currently required to do when deciding whether someone's responsibility was diminished.

CHAPTER 8

Summary

Crimes, and particularly violent crimes, committed by the mentally disordered attract academic and public attention. They raise issues of moral responsibility and public protection. Legal and medical devices, such as diminished responsibility and hospital orders, allow the courts to make special arrangements for the mentally disordered. These devices have been described elsewhere. What have not been described in a systematic way are the principles which led to their development. The first question which I have asked, therefore, is why some people benefit from these devices and some do not.

I have tried to answer the question by examining the principles of justification, excuse and mitigation. A defendant who has been shown to have committed an illegal act can usually have his punishment reduced only where one of these three principles applies. The meanings of the terms were examined first. Justification emerged, I think, as a word which has been employed ambiguously by legal authors over the years. It has been used to assert both that what was done was right and that the defendant believed that he was right to do as he did. The second chapter concluded that the second of these uses in fact describes an excuse.

Excuses refer not to acts themselves, but to the extent to which an actor can be held responsible for an act. Mental factors can influence the ways in which courts deal with mentally disordered offenders by providing partial and complete excuses. I examined several theories of excuse. One, character theory, asserts that an illegal act is excusable when it was out of character for the defendant. The other, choice theory, asserts that a defendant has an excuse when his ability to choose was impaired at the time he acted. I find choice theory more satisfactory. We excuse some people, such as those whose abnormal brain development is a consequence of brain injury or a chromosomal abnormality, when their antisocial behaviour is lifelong. Character theory seems to imply that, since their actions are 'in' character and not 'out' of it, they should be punished like anyone else.

Mitigation is the process whereby the severity of punishment is reduced after conviction. The criteria which courts apply fall into several groups. Three of these have relevance to psychiatry. First, psychiatric factors may provide a partial excuse. Second, psychiatric treatment may be seen as reducing the risk of repetition and the courts may therefore prefer treatment to punishment. Finally, the judge or magistrate may feel that the mentally disordered defendant would suffer unduly in prison.

In the fourth and fifth chapters I explored the psychological and psychiatric aspects of excuses. First, the way in which mental disorder contributes to an excuse by affecting consciousness, emotion, impulsivity, perception, belief or attention were examined. The discussion took place in the light of the conclusion I reached earlier; namely, that an excuse exists where the actor's ability to choose was impaired. Next, I looked at the current legal provision for excusing mentally disordered offenders in England and America. I described the extent to which the automatism defence, the M'Naghten Rules and the American Law Institute test take into account a defendant's responsibility. I concluded that none address the question of whether or not the defendant could make an adequate choice to act as he or she did.

Instead, Anglo-American law has adopted two ways of measuring responsibility. First, it asks whether the defendant suffered from a particular condition, such as 'mental imbalance' in infanticide or 'abnormality of mind' in diminished responsibility. This I described here as the application of a did-he-have-it? test. Alternatively, it asks whether the defendant was capable of performing certain mental functions, such as distinguishing between right and wrong for the purposes of the M'Naghten Rules. This I described here as a could-he-do-it? test. Some legal devices employ one type of test alone. Most, like the insanity defence in England, use both.

I discussed some of the advantages and disadvantages of each type of test. I suggested an alternative approach, one developed from the philosophical writing on the nature of choice. Normal choice requires normal desires and beliefs. Philosophers have pointed out, however, that normal choice also requires the ability to combine those desires and beliefs in a way which reflects their relationship to each other and their importance to the chooser. I have suggested that an improved test of legal responsibility would require the courts to assess not only whether a defendant's desires and beliefs were normal, but also whether he or she was able to order those desires and beliefs in a normal way.

The jury could be asked this in so many words or required to consider only whether the defendant made a 'proper' or an 'adequate' choice to act as he did. Whichever course was adopted, it is likely that a choice-based test would make greater demands on juries than the present law does. Research would be needed to establish whether juries would find these demands excessive. Methods exist to do this. If a choice-based test could not be made to work, I have argued, the proposals of the Butler Committee have the particular merit of reflecting our desire to excuse different people for different reasons at different times.

Cases cited

Two references are provided where the first is difficult to obtain. Page numbers in the text relate to the second reference.

Boardman v. *Woodman* [1865] 47 N.H. 120

Breen v. *Breen* [1961] S.C. 158

Carter v. *United States* [1957] 252 F.2d. 608

Cawthorne v. *HM Advocate* [1968] J.C. 32

Commonwealth v. *Chester* [1958] 150 N.E.2d. 914

Commonwealth v. *Rogers* [1844] 48 Mass. 500; 41 A.D. 458

DPP v. *A. and BC Chewing Gum Ltd.* [1968] 1 Q.B. 159

DPP v. *Camplin* [1978] A.C. 705

DPP v. *Rogers* [1998] Crim.L.R. 202

DPP v. *Smith* [1961] A.C. 290

Davis v. *United States* [1897] 165 U.S. 373

Downs v. *State* [1959] 330 S.W.2d 281

Durham v. *United States* [1954] 214 F.2d 862

Elliot v *C.* [1983] 77 Cr.App.R. 103

Flowers v. *State* [1956] 139 N.E.2d 185

HM Advocate v. *Kidd* [1960] J.C. 61

HM Advocate v. *Dingwall* [1867] 5 Irv.Just. 466

Hill v. *Baxter* [1958] 1 Q.B. 277

Jones v. *US [1983] 103 S.Ct. 3043; 77 L.Ed.2d 694*

London Borough of Southwark v. *Williams and another* [1971] 2 All E.R. 175

Parsons v. *State* [1887] 81 Ala. 577; 60 A.R. 193

People v. *Higgins* [1959] 159 N.E.2d. 179

People v. *Maine* [1901] 59 N.E. 696

People v. *Perkins* [1962] 227 N.Y.S.2d. 663

People v. *Rittger* [1960] 7 Cal.Rptr. 901

People v. *Skinner* [1985] 217 Cal.Rptr. 685

People v. *Young* [1962] 229 N.Y.S.2d. 1

Perka et al. v. *R.* [1984] 13 D.L.R. 1

Phillips v. *R.* [1969] 2 A.C. 130

Pollard v. *United States* [1959] 171 F. Supp. 474

R. v. *Ahluwalia* [1993] 96 Cr.App.R. 133

R. v. *Alderson* [1989] 11 Cr.App.R.(S) 301

R. v. *Alexander* [1913] 9 Cr.App.R. 139

R. v. *Allen and Bennett* [1988] 10 Cr.App.R.(S) 466

R. v. *Arnold* [1724] 16 How. State Tr. 695

R. v. *Backshall* [1998] 1 W.L.R. 1506

R. v. *Barrick* [1985] 7 Cr.App.R.(S) 142

R. v. *Beaumont* [1987] 9 Cr.App.R.(S) 342

R. v. *Beckford* [1988] A.C. 130

R. v. *Bedder* [1954] 2 All E.R. 801

R. v. *Bell* [1984] 3 All E.R. 842

R. v. *Billam* [1986] 82 Cr.App.R. 347

R. v. *Bird* [1987] 9 Cr.App.R.(S) 77

R. v. *Boswell* [1982] 4 Cr.App.R.(S) 317

R. v. *Bourne* [1939] 1 K.B. 687

R. v. *Bratty* [1963] A.C. 386

R. v. *Burgess* [1991] 2 Q.B. 92

R. v. *Burstow* [1998] A.C. 147

R. v. *Byrne* [1960] 2 Q.B. 396

R. v. *Caldwell* [1981] 1 All E.R. 961

R. v. *Chan-Fook* [1994] 99 Cr.App.R. 147

R. v. *Charlson* [1955] 1 All E.R. 859

R. v. *Clarke* [1972] 1 All E.R. 219

R. v. *Clegg* [1995] 2 W.L.R. 80

R. v. *Codere* [1916] 12 Cr.App.Rep. 21

R. v. *Coles* [1995] 1 Cr.App.R. 157

R. v. *Conway* [1989] Q.B. 290

R. v. *Creighton* [1908] 14 Can.Cr.Cas. 349

R. v. *Cunningham* [1957] 2 All E.R. 412

R. v. *Dadson* [1850] 2 Den 35; 169 E.R. 407

R. v. *Dawson* [1987] 9 Cr.App.R.(S) 248

R. v. *Dickie* [1984] 3 All E.R. 173

R. v. *Dudley and Stephens* [1884] 14 Q.B.D. 273

R. v. *Duffy* [1949] 1 All E.R. 932

R. v. *Ford* [1980] 2 Cr.App.R.(S) 33

R. v. *Gladstone Williams* [1984] 78 Cr.App.R. 276

R. v. *Graham* [1982] 74 Cr.App.R. 235

R. v. *Grant* [1990] 12 Cr.App.R.(S) 441

R. v. *Hadfield* [1800] 27 How. State Tr. (New Series) 1281

R. v. *Haleth* [1982] 4 Cr.App.R.(S) 178

R. v. *Harper* [1968] 2 Q.B. 108

R. v. *Haynes* [1859] 1 F. and F. 666; 175 E.R. 898

R. v. *Hayward* [1833] 6 C. and P. 157

R. v. *Stanley and Spindler* [1981] Cr.App.R.(S) 373

R. v. *Stewart* [1987] 9 Cr.App.R.(S) 135

R. v. *Sullivan* [1984] A.C. 156

R. v. *Symonds* [1998] Crim.L.R. 280

R. v. *T.* [1990] Crim.L.R. 256

R. v. *Thornton* [1993] 96 Cr.App.R. 112

R. v. *Turner* [1975] 61 Cr.App.R. 67

R. v. *Turner* [1975] Q.B. 834

R. v. *Varden* [1981] Crim.L.R. 272

R. v. *Vaughan* [1982] 4 Cr.App.R.(S) 83

R. v. *Welsh* [1869] 11 Cox C.C. 336

R. v. *Whybrew* [1979] Crim.L.R. 599

R. v. *Wigley* [1978] Crim.L.R. 635

R. v. *Willer* [1986] 83 Cr.App.Rep. 225

R. v. *Willis* [1974] 60 Cr.App.R. 146

R. v. *Windle* [1952] 2 All E.R. 1

R. v. *Woollin* [1998] 4 All E.R. 103

Rabey v. *R.* [1980] 54 C.C.C.2d. 1

Stapleton v. *R.* [1952] 86 C.L.R. 358

State v. *Andrews* [1961] 357 P.2d 739

State v. *Boan* [1984] 686 P.2d 160

State v. *Foster* [1960] 354 P.2d 960

State v. *Hoyt* [1964] 128 N.W.2d. 645

State v. *Jones* [1871] 50 N.H. 369; 9 A.R. 242

State v. *Pike* [1869] 49 N.H. 399; 6 A.R. 533

US. v. *Holmes* [1842] 26 Fed.Cas. 360

United States v. *Currens* [1961] 290 F.2d. 751

United States v. *Kunak* [1954] 5 C.M.A. 346

United States v. *Segna* [1977] 555 F.2d 226

Wade v. *United States* [1970] 426 F.2d 64

Woolmington v. *DPP* [1935] A.C. 462

References

Abercrombie, J. (1833) *Inquiries Concerning the Intellectual Powers and the Investigation of Truth.* Fourth edition. Edinburgh: Waugh and Innes.

Abrams, S. (1983) 'The multiple personality: A legal defence.' *American Journal of Clinical Hypnosis 25*, 225–231.

Albert, D., Burns, W. and Scheie, H. (1965) 'Severe orbitocranial foreign-body injury.' *American Journal of Ophthalmology 60*, 1109–1111.

Alldridge, P. (1983) 'The coherence of defences.' *Criminal Law Review*, 665–672.

Allen, M. (1997) *Textbook on Criminal Law.* Fourth edition. London: Blackstone.

American Law Institute (1962) *Model Penal Code. Proposed Official Draft.* Philadelphia: American Law Institute.

American Law Institute (1985) *Model Penal Code and Commentaries.* Philadelphia: American Law Institute.

American Psychiatric Association (1994) *Diagnostic and Statistical Manual of Mental Disorders. DSM IV.* Fourth edition. Washington D.C.: American Psychiatric Association.

Anderson, E. (1964) *Psychiatry.* London: Bailliere, Tindall and Cox.

Anthony, H. (1972) *An Experiment in Personality Assessment of Young Men Remanded in Custody. Home Office Research Studies 13.* London: HMSO.

Aranella, P. (1990) 'Character, choice and moral agency.' In E. Paul, F. Miller and J. Paul (eds) *Crime, Culpability and Remedy.* Oxford: Blackwell.

Arieti, S. (1966) 'Schizophrenic cognition.' In P. Hoch and J. Zubin (eds) *Psychopathology of Schizophrenia.* New York: Grune and Stratton.

Aristotle, *Ethica Nicomachea.* Translated (1925) by D. Ross. London: Oxford University Press.

Ashworth, A. (1975) 'Reason, logic and criminal liability.' *Law Quarterly Review 91*, 102–130.

Ashworth, A. (1976) 'The doctrine of provocation.' *Cambridge Law Journal 35*, 292–320.

Ashworth, A. (1983) *Sentencing and Penal Policy.* London: Weidenfeld and Nicholson.

Ashworth, A. (1992) *Sentencing and Criminal Justice.* London: Weidenfeld and Nicholson.

Ashworth, A. (1995a) *Principles of Criminal Law.* Second edition. Oxford: Clarendon.

Ashworth, A. (1995b) *Sentencing and Criminal Justice.* Second edition. London: Weidenfeld and Nicholson.

Asperger, H. (1944) 'Die 'Autistischen Psychopathen' im Kindesalter.' *Archiv für Psychiatrie und Nervenkrankheiten 117*, 76–136.

Austin, J. (1956–57) 'A plea for excuses.' *Proceedings of the Aristotelean Society 57*, 1–30.

Banks, W. and Prinzmetal, W. (1976) 'Configurational effects in visual information processing.' *Perception and Psychophysics 19*, 361–367.

Baron-Cohen, S., Leslie, A. and Frith, U. (1985) 'Does the autistic child have a "theory of mind"?' *Cognition 21*, 37–46.

Barras, V. and Bernheim, J. (1990) 'The history of law and psychiatry in Europe.' In R. Bluglass and P. Bowden (eds) *Principles and Practice of Forensic Psychiatry.* Edinburgh: Churchill Livingstone.

Bauer, R. (1982) 'Visual hypoemotionality as a symptom of visual-limbic disconnection in man.' *Archives of Neurology 39*, 702–708.

Bayles, M. (1982) 'Character, purpose and criminal responsibility.' *Law and Philosophy 1*, 5–20.

Bazelon, D. (1974) 'Psychiatrists and the adversary process.' *Scientific American 230*, 6, 18–23.

Beaumont, J. (1821) 'An essay on criminal jurisprudence.' *The Pamphleteer 18*, 67–80, 402–432; *19*, 97–133.

Beaumont, M. (1988) 'Psychiatric evidence: Over-rationalising the abnormal.' *Criminal Law Review*, 290–294.

Beck, A., Rush, J., Shaw, B. and Emery, G. (1979) *Cognitive Therapy of Depression.* New York: Guilford Press.

Beigel, A. and Murphy, D. (1971) 'Assessing clinical characteristics of the manic state.' *American Journal of Psychiatry 128*, 688–694.

Bentham, J. (1823) *An Introduction to the Principles of Morals and Legislation, Volumes One and Two.* Second edition. London: Pickering.

Bentham, J. (1843) *The Works of Jeremy Bentham, Volume Ten.* Edinburgh: William Tait.

Blackburn, R. (1988) 'On moral judgements and personality disorders.' *British Journal of Psychiatry 153*, 505–512.

Blackstone, W. (1769) *Commentaries on the Laws of England, Volume Four.* Oxford: Clarendon.

Bleuler, E. (1911) *Dementia Praecox oder die Gruppe der Schizophrenien.* Translated (1950) by J. Zinkin as *Dementia Praecox or the Group of Schizophrenias.* London: George Allen.

Bleuler, E. (1924) *Textbook of Psychiatry.* Translated by A. Brill. New York: Macmillan.

Bluglass, R. (1990) 'Infanticide and filicide.' In R. Bluglass and P. Bowden (eds) *Principles and Practice of Forensic Psychiatry.* Edinburgh: Churchill Livingstone.

Bonnie, R. and Slobogin, C. (1980) 'The role of mental health professionals in the criminal process: The case for informed speculation.' *Virginia Law Review 66*, 427–522.

Bosch, G. (1962) *Monographien aus dem Gesamtgebiete der Neurologie und Psychiatrie.* Translated (1970) by D. Jordan and I. Jordan as *Infantile Autism.* Berlin: Springer-Verlag.

Bracton, H. (1640) *De Legibus et Consuetudinibus Angliae.* London: Flesher and Young.

Bregman, A. and Campbell, J. (1971) 'Primary auditory stream segregation and perception of order in a rapid sequences of tones.' *Journal of Experimental Psychology 89*, 244–249.

Brett, P. (1963) *An Inquiry into Criminal Guilt.* London: Sweet and Maxwell.

Briscoe, O. (1975) 'Intention at the moment of crime ... beyond reasonable doubt?' *Medicine, Science and the Law 15*, 42–46.

Buchanan, A. (1993) 'Acting on delusion: A review.' *Psychological Medicine 23*, 123–134.

Buchanan, A., Reed, A., Wessely, S., Garety, P., Taylor, P., Grubin, D. and Dunn, G. (1993) 'Acting on delusions II: The phenomenological correlates of acting on delusions.' *British Journal of Psychiatry 163*, 77–81.

Bucknill, J. (1884) 'A lecture on the relation of madness to crime.' *British Medical Journal*, 499–502.

Butler, S. (1872) *Erewhon.* London: Trubner and Co.

Callahan, L., Mayer, C. and Steadman, H. (1987) 'Insanity defense reform in the United States – post Hinckley.' *Mental and Physical Disability Law Reporter 11*, 54–59.

Cardozo, B. (1947) *Selected Writings.* Edited by M. Hall. New York: Fallon.

Carlson, E. and Simpson, M. (1965) 'Benjamin Rush's medical use of the moral faculty.' *Bulletin of the History of Medicine 39*, 22–33.

Carlson, G. and Goodwin, F. (1973) 'The stages of mania: A longitudinal analysis of the manic episode.' *Archives of General Psychiatry 28*, 221–228.

Cegalis, J., Leen, D. and Solomon, E. (1977) 'Attention in schizophrenia: An analysis of selectivity in functional visual field.' *Journal of Abnormal Psychology 86*, 470–482.

Clarkson, C. and Keating, H. (1998) *Criminal Law: Text and Materials*. Fourth edition. London: Sweet and Maxwell.

Cleckley, H. (1964) *The Mask of Sanity: An Attempt to Clarify Issues about the So-Called Psychopathic Personality*. Fourth edition. St. Louis: Mosby.

Cohen, L. (1977) *The Probable and the Provable*. Oxford: Clarendon.

Collett, P. (1977) 'The rules of conduct.' In P. Collett (ed.) *Social Rules and Social Behaviour*. Oxford: Basil Blackwell.

Committee on Insanity and Crime (Atkin Committee) (1924) Report. Cmnd. 2005. London: HMSO.

Committee on Mentally Abnormal Offenders (Butler Committee) (1975) Report. Cmnd. 6244. London: HMSO.

Conrad, K. (1958) *Die Beginnende Schizophrenie*. Stuttgart: G. Thieme.

Cox, E. (1877) *Principles of Punishment*. London: Times Law Office.

Craig, T. (1982) 'An epidemiologic study of problems associated with violence among psychiatric inpatients.' *American Journal of Psychiatry 139*, 1262–1266.

Crane, D. (1976) 'More violent Capgras.' *American Journal of Psychiatry 133*, 1350.

Criminal Law Revision Committee (1980) *Fourteenth Report: Offences against the Person*. Cmnd. 7844. London: HMSO.

Cutting, J. (1985) *The Psychology of Schizophrenia*. Edinburgh: Churchill Livingstone.

D'Arcy, E. (1963) *Human Acts*. Oxford: Clarendon.

D'Orban, P. (1979) 'Women who kill their children.' *British Journal of Psychiatry 134*, 560–571.

Davidson, D. (1980) *Essays on Actions and Events*. Oxford: Clarendon.

De Ajuriaguerra, J., Strejilevitch, M. and Tissot, R. (1963) 'A propos de quelques conduites devant le miroir de sujets atteints de syndromes dementiels du grand age.' *Neuropsychologia 1*, 59–73.

Dell, S. (1984) *Murder into Manslaughter*. Maudsley Monograph Number 27. Oxford: Oxford University Press.

Dennett, D. (1969) *Content and Consciousness*. London: Routledge and Kegan Paul.

Dennett, D. (1973) 'Mechanism and responsibility.' In T. Honderich (ed.) *Essays on Freedom of Action*. London: Routledge and Kegan Paul.

Denning, A. (1953) *The Changing Law*. London: Stevens and Sons.

Descartes, R. (1637) *Discours de la Methode*. Translated (1985) by R. Stoothoff as *Discourse on the Method*. In J. Cottingham, R. Stoothoff and D. Murdoch (eds) *The Philosophical Writings of Descartes Volume One*. Cambridge: Cambridge University Press.

Dougherty, F., Bartlett, E. and Izard, C. (1974) 'Responses of schizophrenics to expressions of the fundamental emotions.' *Journal of Clinical Psychology 30*, 243–246.

Dressler, J. (1988) 'Provocation: Partial justification or partial excuse?' *Modern Law Review 51*, 467–480.

Drewe, E (1973) *An Experimental Investigation of Deficits Found following Lesions in the Frontal Lobes*. Thesis for PhD, University of London.

Duff, R. (1990) *Intention, Agency and Criminal Liability*. Oxford: Basil Blackwell.

Duff, R. (1993) 'Choice, character and criminal liability.' *Law and Philosophy 12*, 345–383.

Eichelberger, E. (1984) 'Automatism or unconsciousness as defense to criminal charge.' *American Law Reports 4th Series 27*, 1067–1143.

Elliot, C. (1991) 'The rules of insanity: A commentary on psychopathic disorder: A category mistake.' *Journal of Medical Ethics 17*, 89–90.

Eser, A. (1976) 'Justification and excuse.' *American Journal of Comparative Law 24*, 621–637.

Esquirol, E. (1845) *Mental Maladies.* Translated by E. Hunt. Philadelphia: Lea and Blanchard.

Feinberg, J. (1970) *Doing and Deserving.* Princeton: Princeton University Press.

Feldstein, S. (1962) 'The relationship of interpersonal involvement and affectiveness of content to the verbal communication of schizophrenic patients.' *Journal of Abnormal and Social Psychology 64*, 39–45.

Fenwick, P. (1990) 'Automatism.' In R. Bluglass and P. Bowden (eds) *Principles and Practice of Forensic Psychiatry.* Edinburgh: Churchill Livingstone.

Ferracuti, S. (1996) 'Cesare Lombroso (1835–1907).' *Journal of Forensic Psychiatry 7*, 130–149.

Fey, E. (1951) 'The performance of young schizophrenics and young normals on the Wisconsin card-sorting test.' *Journal of Consulting Psychology 15*, 311–319.

Fingarette, H. (1972) *The Meaning of Criminal Insanity.* Berkeley: University of California Press.

Fingarette, H. and Fingarette Hasse, A. (1979) *Mental Disabilities and Criminal Responsibility.* Berkeley: University of California Press.

Fisse, B. (1990) *Howard's Criminal Law.* Fifth edition. Sydney: The Law Book Company.

Fletcher, G. (1974) 'The individualization of excusing conditions.' *Southern California Law Review 47*, 1269–1309.

Fletcher, G. (1978) *Rethinking Criminal Law.* Boston: Little, Brown.

Fletcher, G. (1979) 'Should intolerable prison conditions generate a justification or an excuse for escape?' *University of California Los Angeles Law Review 26*, 1355–1369.

Fonseca, J., Gil, M., Figueira, M., Barata, J., Pego, F. and Pacheco, M. (1978) 'How do normal subjects learn a simple adaptive task: How and why do paranoid schizophrenics fail?' *Archiv für Psychiatrie und Nervenkrankheiten 225*, 31–53.

Foucault, M. (1961) *Histoire de la Folie.* Translated (1965) by R. Howard as *Madness and Civilization.* London: Tavistock.

Fox, S. (1963) 'Physical disorder, consciousness and criminal liability.' *Columbia Law Review 63*, 645–668.

Frances, A., First, M., Widiger, T., Miele, G., Tilly, S., Davis, W. and Pincus, H. (1991) 'An A–Z guide to DSM-IV conundrums.' *Journal of Abnormal Psychology 100*, 407–412.

Frankfurt, H. (1971) 'Freedom of the will and the concept of a person.' *Journal of Philosophy 68*, 5–20.

Frankfurt, H. (1987) 'Identification and wholeheartedness.' In F. Schoeman (ed.) *Responsibility, Character and the Emotions.* Cambridge: Cambridge University Press.

Frederiks, J. (1969) 'The agnosias. Disorders of perceptual recognition.' In P. Vinken and G. Bruyn (eds) *Handbook of Clinical Neurology, Volume Four.* Amsterdam: North-Holland.

Freedman, B. (1974) 'The subjective experience of perceptual and cognitive disturbances in schizophrenia: A review of autobiographical accounts.' *Archives of General Psychiatry 30*, 333–340.

Freedman, B. and Chapman, L. (1973) 'Early subjective experience in schizophrenic episodes.' *Journal of Abnormal Psychology 82*, 46–54.

French, A. and Shechmeister, B. (1983) 'The multiple personality syndrome and criminal defense.' *Bulletin of the American Academy of Psychiatry and the Law 11*, 17–25.

Freud, S. (1916) 'The premises and technique of interpretation.' In S. Freud (1971) *The Complete Introductory Lectures on Psychoanalysis.* Translated and edited by J. Strachey. London: George Allen and Unwin.

Fulford, K. (1989) *Moral Theory and Medical Practice*. Cambridge: Cambridge University Press.

Garcon, E. (1901) *Code Penal Annote. Tome Premier*. Second edition (1952) edited by M. Rousselet, M. Patin and M. Ancel. Paris: Sirey.

Garety, P. and Helmsley, D. (1987) 'Characteristics of delusional experience.' *European Archives of Psychiatry and Neurological Sciences 236*, 294–298.

Garland, D. (1990) *Punishment and Modern Society*. Oxford: Clarendon.

Garmezy, N. (1978) 'Attentional processes in adult schizophrenia and in children at risk.' *Journal of Psychiatric Research 14*, 3–34.

Gelder, M., Gath, D. and Mayou, R. (1983) *Oxford Textbook of Psychiatry*. Oxford: Oxford University Press.

Gillet, G. (1986) 'Multiple personality and the concept of a person.' *New Ideas in Psychology 4*, 173–184.

Glazebrook, P. (1972) 'The necessity plea in English criminal law.' *Cambridge Law Journal 30*, 87–119.

Glueck, B. (1919) 'Book review.' *Mental Hygiene 3*, 157–166.

Glueck, S. (1963) *Law and Psychiatry*. London: Tavistock.

Goldstein, A. (1967) *The Insanity Defense*. New Haven: Yale University Press.

Goldstein, J. and Katz, J. (1963) 'Abolish the insanity defense – why not?' *Yale Law Journal 72*, 853–876.

Gordon, G. (1978) *The Criminal Law of Scotland*. Second edition. Edinburgh: W. Green and Son.

Green, B., Wilson, J. and Lindy, J. (1985) 'Conceptualizing post-traumatic stress disorder: A psychosocial framework.' In C. Figley (ed.) *Trauma and Its Wake*. New York: Brunner-Mazel.

Greenawalt, K. (1984) 'The perplexing borders of justification and excuse.' *Columbia Law Review 84*, 1897–1927.

Greenawalt, K. (1987) *Conflicts of Law and Morality*. New York: Oxford University Press.

Greilsheimer, H. and Groves, J. (1979) 'Male genital self-mutilation.' *Archives of General Psychiatry 36*, 441–446.

Griew, E. (1988) 'The future of diminished responsibility.' *Criminal Law Review*, 75–87.

Gross, H. (1979) *A Theory of Criminal Justice*. New York: Oxford University Press.

Guarnieri, P. (1993) *A Case of Child Murder: Law and Science in Nineteenth-Century Tuscany*. Cambridge: Polity Press.

Gunn, J. and Fenton, G. (1971) 'Epilepsy, automatism and crime.' *The Lancet 1*, 1173–1176.

Gunn, J. and Robertson, G. (1976) 'Psychopathic personality: A conceptual problem.' *Psychological Medicine 6*, 631–634.

Gunn, J. and Taylor, P. (1993) *Forensic Psychiatry: Clinical, Legal and Ethical Issues*. Oxford: Butterworth Heinemann.

Gunn, J., Maden, A. and Swinton, M. (1991) 'Treatment needs of prisoners with psychiatric disorders.' *British Medical Journal 303*, 338–341.

Guttmacher, M. and Weihofen, H. (1952) *Psychiatry and the Law*. New York: Norton.

Hafner, H. and Boker, W. (1973) *Gewalttaten Geistesgestorter*. Translated (1982) by H. Marshall as *Crimes of Violence by Mentally Abnormal Offenders*. Cambridge: Cambridge University Press.

Hale, M. (1736) *Historia Placitorum Coronae, Volumes One and Two*. London: Gyles, Woodward, Davis.

Hall, J. (1947) *General Principles of Criminal Law*. Second edition. Indianapolis: Bobbs-Merrill Co.

Hall, J. (1956) 'Psychiatry and criminal responsibility.' *Yale Law Journal 65*, 761–785.

Hall, J., George, B. and Force, R. (1976) *Criminal Law and Procedure*. Third edition. Indianapolis: Bobbs-Merrill.

Halleck, S. (1990) 'Dissociative phenomena and the question of responsibility.' *International Journal of Clinical and Experimental Hypnosis 38*, 298–314.

Hamilton, M. (1985) *Fish's Clinical Psychopathology*. Second edition. Bristol: Wright.

Hart, B. (1912) *The Psychology of Insanity*. London: Cambridge University Press.

Hart, H. (1968) *Punishment and Responsibility*. Oxford: Clarendon Press.

Hartmann, H. (1925) 'Self-mutilation.' *Jahrbuch fur Psychiatrie und Neurologie 44*, 31. Abstracted in *Archives of Neurology and Psychiatry 15*, 384–386.

Hawkins, H. (1787) *A Treatise of the Pleas of the Crown, Volumes One and Two*. London: Thomas Whieldon.

Hill, D. (1952) 'EEG in episodic psychotic and psychopathic behaviour: A classification of data.' *Electroencephalography and Clinical Neurophysiology 4*, 419–442.

Hinton, J. and Withers, E. (1971) 'The usefulness of the clinical tests of the sensorium.' *British Journal of Psychiatry 119*, 9–18.

Hoch, A. and Kirby, G. (1919) 'A clinical study of psychoses characterized by distressed perplexity.' *Archives of Neurology and Psychiatry 1*, 415–458.

Hoffbauer, J. (1808) *Die Psychologie in Ihren Hauptanwendungen auf die Rechtspflege*. Halle: Schimmelpfennig.

Holdsworth, W. (1956) *A History of English Law, Volume One*. Seventh edition. London: Methuen.

Holmes, C. (1991) 'Psychopathic disorder: A category mistake?' *Journal of Medical Ethics 17*, 77–85.

Holmes, O. (1881) *The Common Law*. Boston: Little, Brown.

Horder, J. (1992) *Provocation and Responsibility*. Oxford: Clarendon.

Hume, D. (1739) *A Treatise on Human Nature, Book One*. Edited (1888) by L. Selby-Bigge. Oxford: Clarendon.

Hume, D. (1748) *Philosophical Essays Concerning Human Understanding*. London: Millar.

Hume, D. (1800) *Commentaries on the Laws of Scotland Respecting Crimes, Volume One*. Reprinted 1986. Edinburgh: Law Society of Scotland.

Husak, D. (1992) 'The serial view of criminal law defenses.' *Criminal Law Forum 3*, 369–400.

Hwu, H-G., Chen, C-C., Tsuang, M. and Tseng, W-S. (1981) 'Derealization syndrome and the outcome of schizophrenia: A report from the International Pilot Study of Schizophrenia.' *British Journal of Psychiatry 139*, 313–318.

Insanity Defense Work Group (1983) 'American Psychiatric Association statement on the insanity defense.' *American Journal of Psychiatry 140*, 681–688.

James, W. (1891) *The Principles of Psychology, Volume One*. London: Macmillan.

Jones, I. (1965) 'Observations on schizophrenic stereotypies.' *Comprehensive Psychiatry 6*, 323–335.

Kadish, S. (1987) 'Excusing crime.' *California Law Review 75*, 257–289.

Kanner, L. (1943) 'Autistic disturbances of affective contact.' *The Nervous Child 2*, 217–250.

Kant, E. (1781) *Kritik der Reinen Vernunft*. Translated (1929) by N. Smith as *Critique of Pure Reason*. London: Macmillan.

Kant, E. (1788) *Kritik der Praktischen Vernunft*. Translated (1898) by T. Abbott as *Critique of Practical Reason*. London: Longmans.

Katz, D. (1951) *Gestalt Psychology*. London: Methuen.

Keane, T., Fairbank, J., Caddell, J., Zimering, R. and Bender, M. (1985) 'A behavioral approach to assessing and treating post-traumatic stress disorder in Vietnam veterans.' In C. Figley (ed.) *Trauma and Its Wake.* New York: Brunner-Mazel.

Kendell, R. and Zealley, A. (1993) *Companion to Psychiatric Studies.* Fifth edition. Edinburgh: Churchill Livingstone.

Kenny, A. (1978) *Freewill and Responsibility.* London: Routledge and Kegan Paul.

Klein, D. (1984) *The Concept of Consciousness.* Lincoln: University of Nebraska Press.

Kleist, K. (1928) 'Cycloid, paranoid and epileptoid psychoses and the problem of the degenerative psychoses.' Reprinted in S. Hirsch and M. Shepherd (eds) (1974) *Themes and Variations in European Psychiatry.* Bristol: Wright.

Kluft, R. (1987) 'An update on multiple personality disorder.' *Hospital and Community Psychiatry* 38, 363–373.

Koffka, K. (1950) *Principles of Gestalt Psychology.* London: Routledge and Kegan Paul.

Kornetsky, C. and Orzack, M. (1978) 'Physiological and behavioural correlates of attention dysfunction in schizophrenic patients.' *Journal of Psychiatric Research 14,* 69–79.

Kraepelin, E. (1913) *Psychiatrie, Volume 3, Part 2.* Eighth edition. Translated (1919) by M. Barclay as *Dementia Praecox and Paraphrenia.* Edinburgh: Livingstone.

Krakowski, M., Volavka, J. and Brizer, D. (1986) 'Psychopathology and violence: A review of literature.' *Comprehensive Psychiatry 27,* 131–148.

Kretschmer, E. (1961) *Hysteria, Reflex and Instinct.* Translated by V. Baskin and W. Baskin. London: Peter Owen.

Kupperman, J. (1978) *Philosophy: The Fundamental Problems.* New York: St Martin's Press.

LEGE (1844) 'The punishment of death.' *The Zoist 2,* 295–316.

Lacey, N. (1988) *State Punishment.* London: Routledge.

LaFave, W. and Scott, A. (1972) *Criminal Law.* St. Paul: West Publishing Company.

Langfeldt, G. (1960) 'Diagnosis and prognosis of schizophrenia.' *Proceedings of the Royal Society of Medicine 53,* 1047–1052.

Law Commission (1985) *No. 143. Codification of the Criminal Law.* London: HMSO.

Law Commission (1989) *No. 177. Criminal Law. A Criminal Code for England and Wales, Volumes One and Two.* London: HMSO.

Leonhard, K. (1957) *Aufteilung der Endogenen Psychosen.* Translated (1979) by R. Berman as *The Classification of Endogenous Psychoses.* Fifth edition. New York: Halsted Press.

Lewis, A. (1974) 'Psychopathic personality: A most elusive category.' *Psychological Medicine 4,* 133–140.

Lishman, A. (1978) *Organic Psychiatry.* Oxford: Blackwell.

Lloyd, M. and Bénézech, M. (1991) 'Criminal responsibility in the French judicial system.' *Journal of Forensic Psychiatry 2,* 281–294.

Locke, J. (1690) *An Essay Concerning Human Understanding.* Edited (1975) by P. Nidditch. Oxford: Clarendon.

Ludolph, P. (1985) 'How prevalent is multiple personality?' *American Journal of Psychiatry 142,* 1526–1527.

Luria, A. (1980) *Higher Cortical Functions in Man.* Second edition. London: Basic Books.

Luria, A. and Homskaya, E. (1964) 'Disturbance in the regulative role of speech with frontal lobe lesions.' In J. Warren and K. Akert (eds) *The Frontal Granular Cortex and Behaviour.* New York: McGraw Hill.

Luria, A., Karpov, B. and Yarbuss, A. (1966) 'Disturbances of active visual perception with lesions of the frontal lobes.' *Cortex 2,* 202–212.

Macalpine, I. and Hunter, R. (1969) *George III and the Mad-Business*. London: Allen Lane.

Mackay, R. (1988) 'Post-Hinckley insanity in the USA.' *Criminal Law Review*, 88–96.

Mackay, R. (1990) 'Fact and fiction about the insanity defence.' *Criminal Law Review*, 247–255.

Mackay, R. (1995) *Mental Condition Defences in the Criminal Law*. Oxford: Clarendon.

Mackay, R. and Colman, A. (1996) 'Equivocal rulings on expert psychological and psychiatric evidence: Turning a muddle into a nonsense.' *Criminal Law Review*, 88–95.

Magaro, P. and Page, J. (1982) 'Icon thresholds in paranoid and non-paranoid schizophrenics.' *British Journal of Clinical Psychology 21*, 213–219.

Marks, I. (1987) *Fears, Phobias and Rituals*. New York: Oxford University Press.

Maudsley, H. (1897) *Responsibility in Mental Disease*. New York: Appleton.

Mawson, D. (1990) 'Specific defences to a criminal charge: Assessment for court.' In R. Bluglass and P. Bowden (eds) *Principles and Practice of Forensic Psychiatry*. Edinburgh: Churchill Livingstone.

Mawson, D., Grounds, A. and Tantum, D. (1985) 'Violence and Asperger's syndrome: A case study.' *British Journal of Psychiatry 147*, 566–569.

Mayer-Gross, W. (1924) *Selbstschilderungen der Verwirrtheit: Die Oneiroide Erlebnisform*. Berlin: Springer-Verlag.

Mayer-Gross, W. (1935) 'On depersonalization.' *British Journal of Medical Psychology 15*, 103–126.

Mayer-Gross, W., Slater, E. and Roth, M. (1960) *Clinical Psychiatry*. London: Cassell and Co.

McAuley, F. (1987) 'Anticipating the past: The defence of provocation in Irish law.' *Modern Law Review 50*, 133–157.

McAuley, F. (1993) *Insanity, Psychiatry and Criminal Responsibility*. Dublin: Round Hall.

McEvoy, J., Apperson, L., Appelbaum, P., Ortlip, P., Brecosky, J., Hammill, K., Geller, J. and Roth, L. (1989) 'Insight in schizophrenia: Its relationship to acute psychopathology.' *Journal of Nervous and Mental Disease 177*, 43–47.

McGhie, A. and Chapman, J. (1961) 'Disorders of attention and perception in early schizophrenia.' *British Journal of Medical Psychology 34*, 103–116.

McGinn, C. (1979) 'Action and its explanation.' In N. Bolton (ed.) *Philosophical Problems In Psychology*. London: Methuen.

McGreevy, M., Steadman, H. and Callahan, L. (1991) 'The negligible effects of California's 1982 reform of the insanity defence test.' *American Journal of Psychiatry 148*, 744–750.

Merskey, H. (1979) *The Analysis of Hysteria*. London: Bailliere Tindall.

Miller, F. and Chabrier, L. (1988) 'Suicide attempts correlate with delusional content in major depression.' *Psychopathology 21*, 34–37.

Milner, B. (1963) 'Effects of different brain lesions on card sorting.' *Archives of Neurology 9*, 90–100.

Moore, M. (1984) *Law and Psychiatry. Rethinking the Relationship*. Cambridge: Cambridge University Press.

Moore, M. (1990) 'Choice, character and excuse.' In E. Paul, F. Miller and J. Paul (eds) *Crime, Culpability and Remedy*. Oxford: Blackwell.

Morris, N. (1982) *Madness and the Criminal Law*. Chicago: University of Chicago Press.

Morris, N. and Burt, R. (1972) 'A proposal for the abolition of the incompetency plea.' *University of Chicago Law Review 40*, 66–95.

Morse, S. (1979) 'Diminished capacity: A moral and legal conundrum.' *International Journal of Law and Psychiatry 2*, 271–298.

Moxon, D. (1988) *Sentencing Practice in the Crown Court.* Home Office Research Study No. 103. London: HMSO.

Mullen, P. (1988) 'Violence and mental disorder.' *British Journal of Hospital Medicine 40,* 460–463.

Muzekari, L. and Bates, M. (1977) 'Judgement of emotion among chronic schizophrenics.' *Journal of Clinical Psychology 33,* 662–666.

Neale, J., McIntyre, C., Fox, R. and Cromwell, R. (1969) 'Span of apprehension in acute schizophrenics.' *Journal of Abnormal Psychology 74,* 593–596.

Nicolson, D. and Sanghvi, R. (1993) 'Battered women and provocation: The implications of R. v. Ahluwalia.' *Criminal Law Review,* 728–738.

Oken, D., Heath, H., Shipman, W., Goldstein, I., Grinker, R. and Fisch, J. (1966) 'The specificity of responses to stressful stimuli.' *Archives of General Psychiatry 15,* 624–634.

Oppenheimer, H. (1909) *The Criminal Responsibility of Lunatics.* London: Sweet and Maxwell.

Pactet, F. and Colin, H. (1901) *Les Alienes Devant la Justice.* Paris: Masson.

Palmer, J. (1779) *Observations in Defence of the Liberty of Man as a Moral Agent.* London: J. Johnson.

Pastore, N. (1952) 'The role of arbitrariness in the frustration–aggression hypothesis.' *Journal of Abnormal and Social Psychology 47,* 728–731.

Patient, I. (1968) 'Some remarks about the element of voluntariness in offences of absolute liability.' *Criminal Law Review,* 23–32.

Penfield, W. and Jasper, H. (1954) *Epilepsy and the Functional Anatomy of the Human Brain.* London: J. and A. Churchill.

Perris, C. (1974) 'A study of cycloid psychosis.' *Acta Psychiatrica Scandinavica,* Supplement 253.

Pichot, P. (1978) 'Psychopathic behaviour: A historical review.' In R. Hare and D. Schalling (eds) *Psychopathic Behaviour: Approaches to Research.* Chichester: Wiley.

Planck, M. (1933) *Where is Science Going?* London: George Allen and Unwin.

Planck, M. (1950) *Scientific Autobiography and Other Papers.* Translated by F. Gaynor. London: Williams and Norgate.

Posner, M. and Boies, S. (1971) 'Components of attention.' *Psychological Review 78,* 391–408.

Prichard, J. (1842) *On the Different Forms of Insanity in Relation to Jurisprudence.* London: Hippolyte Bailliere.

Priestley, J. (1777) *The Doctrine of Philosophical Necessity Illustrated.* London: J. Johnson.

Prince, M. (1905) *The Dissociation of a Personality.* New York: Longmans, Green.

Prinzmetal, W. and Banks, W. (1977) 'Good continuation affects visual detection.' *Perception and Psychophysics 21,* 389–395.

Radden, J. (1985) *Madness and Reason.* London: George Allen and Unwin.

Radford, J. and Kelly, L. (1995) 'Self-preservation: Feminist activism and feminist jurisprudence.' In M. Maynard and J. Purvis (eds) *(Hetero)sexual Politics.* London: Taylor and Francis.

Radzinowicz, L. (1948) *A History of English Criminal Law. Volume One.* London: Stevens.

Radzinowicz, L. and Turner, J. (1945) *The Modern Approach to Criminal Law.* London: Macmillan.

Ray, I. (1839) *Medical Jurisprudence of Insanity.* London: Henderson.

Raz, J. (1975) *Practical Reason and Norms.* London: Hutchinson.

Reich, S. and Cutting, J. (1982) 'Picture perception and abstract thought in schizophrenia.' *Psychological Medicine 12,* 91–96.

Reik, L. (1953) 'The Doe–Ray correspondence: A pioneer collaboration in the jurisprudence of mental disease.' *Yale Law Journal 63,* 183–196.

Renton, A. (1886) *Monomanie Sans Delire. An Examination of the Irresistible Criminal Impulse Theory.* Edinburgh: T. and T. Clark.

Richardson, P. (ed.) (1999) *Archbold. Criminal Pleading, Evidence and Practice.* 1999 edition. London: Sweet and Maxwell.

Roberts, P. (1996) 'Will you stand up in court? On the admissibility of psychiatric and psychological evidence.' *Journal of Forensic Psychiatry 7,* 63–78.

Robinson, P. (1982) 'Criminal law defenses: A systematic analysis.' *Columbia Law Review 82,* 199–291.

Romanik, R. and Snow, S. (1984) 'Two cases of Capgras' syndrome.' *American Journal of Psychiatry 141,* 720.

Romilly, E. (1810) *Observations on the Criminal Law of England.* London: Cadell and Davies.

Rose, L. (1986) *The Massacre of the Innocents: Infanticide in Britain, 1800–1939.* London: Routledge.

Roth, M. (1971) 'Classification and aetiology in mental disorders of old age: Some recent developments.' In D. Kay and A. Walk (eds) *Recent Developments in Psychogeriatrics.* Ashford: Headley Brothers.

Royal Commission on Capital Punishment (Gowers Commission) (1953) Report. Cmnd 8932. London: HMSO.

Royal Commission on the Law Relating to Mental Illness and Mental Deficiency (1957) Report. Cmnd. 169. London: HMSO.

Ruggles-Brise, E. (1901) *Report to the Secretary of State for the Home Department on the Proceedings of the Fifth and Sixth International Penitentiary Congress.* Cmnd. 573. London: HMSO.

Russell, W. (1819) *A Treatise on Crimes and Misdemeanours, Volume One.* London: Butterworth.

Rutter, M. and Hersov, L. (1985) *Child and Adolescent Psychiatry: Modern Approaches.* London: Blackwell.

Rutter, M. and Schopler, E. (1987) 'Autism and pervasive developmental disorders: Concepts and diagnostic issues.' *Journal of Autism and Developmental Disorders 17,* 159–186.

Scadding, J. (1990) 'The semantic problems of psychiatry.' *Psychological Medicine 20,* 243–248.

Schilder, P. (1935) *The Image and Appearance of the Human Body.* London: Kegan Paul, Trench, Trubner and Co.

Schipkowensky, N. (1968) 'Affective disorders: Cyclophrenia and murder.' In A. Reuck and R. Porter (eds) *The Mentally Abnormal Offender.* London: Churchill.

Schneider, S. (1976) 'Selective attention in schizophrenia.' *Journal of Abnormal Psychology 85,* 167–173.

Schopp, R. (1991) *Automatism, Insanity and the Psychology of Criminal Responsibility.* Cambridge: Cambridge University Press.

Scott, W. (1958) 'Research definitions of mental health and mental illness.' *Psychological Bulletin 55,* 29–45.

Scruton, R. (1994) *Modern Philosophy: A Survey.* London: Sinclair-Stevenson.

Shakow, D. (1950) 'Some psychological features of schizophrenia.' In M. Reymert (ed.) *Feelings and Emotions.* New York: McGraw Hill.

Shapland, J. (1981) *Between Conviction and Sentence.* London: Routledge and Kegan Paul.

Shore, D. (1979) 'Self-mutilation and schizophrenia.' *Comprehensive Psychiatry 20,* 384–387.

Simon, R. (1967) *The Jury and the Defense of Insanity.* Boston: Little, Brown.

Simpson, A. (1984) *Cannibalism and the Common Law.* Chicago: University of Chicago Press.

Slater, E. (1954) 'The M'Naghten Rules and modern concepts of responsibility.' *British Medical Journal,* 713–718.

Slobogin, C. (1985) 'The guilty but mentally ill verdict: An idea whose time should not have come.' *George Washington Law Review 53*, 494–527.

Smith, J. (1989) *Justification and Excuse in the Criminal Law*. London: Stevens and Sons.

Smith, J. (1993) 'Commentary.' *Criminal Law Review*, 958–959.

Smith, J. and Hogan, B. (1992) *Textbook of Criminal Law*. Seventh edition. London: Butterworths.

Smith, J. and Hogan, B. (1996) *Textbook of Criminal Law*. Eighth edition. London: Butterworths.

Sparks, R. (1964) '"Diminished Responsibility" in theory and practice.' *Modern Law Review*, 9–34.

Spohn, H., Thetford, P. and Woodham, F. (1970) 'Span of apprehension and arousal in schizophrenia.' *Journal of Abnormal Psychology 75*, 113–123.

Stengel, E. (1943) 'Further studies on pathological wandering.' *Journal of Mental Science 89*, 224–241.

Stephen, J. (1883) *A History of the Criminal Law of England, Volume Two*. London: Macmillan.

Storring, G. (1939) 'Perplexity.' In J. Cutting and M. Shepherd (eds) (1987) *The Clinical Roots of the Schizophrenia Concept*. Cambridge: Cambridge University Press.

Straube, E. (1975) 'Experimente zur Wahrnehmung Schizophrener.' *Archiv fur Psychiatrie und Nervenkrankheiten 220*, 139–158.

Sullivan, G. (1996) 'Making excuses.' In A. Simester and A. Smith (eds) *Harm and Culpability*. Oxford: Clarendon.

Teuber, H-L. (1964) 'The riddle of frontal lobe function in man.' In J. Warren and K. Akert (eds) *The Frontal Granular Cortex and Behaviour*. New York: McGraw Hill.

Thigpen, C. and Cleckley, H. (1957) *The Three Faces of Eve*. London: Secker and Warburg.

Thomas, D. (1978) *The Penal Equation*. Cambridge: Institute of Criminology.

Thomas, D. (1979a) *Constraints on Judgement*. Cambridge: Institute of Criminology.

Thomas, D. (1979b) *Principles of Sentencing*. Second edition. London: Heinemann.

Thomas, D. (1983) 'Sentencing discretion and appellate review.' In J. Shapland (ed.) *Decision-Making in the Legal System. Issues in Criminological and Legal Psychology*. Occasional Paper No. 5. Leicester: British Psychological Society.

Thomas, D. (1993) *Current Sentencing Practice*. London: Sweet and Maxwell.

Thorpe, B. (1840) *Ancient Laws and Institutes of England, Volume Two*. London: The Commissioners of the Public Records.

Tur, R. (1993) 'Subjectivism and objectivism: Towards synthesis.' In S. Shute, J. Gardner and J. Horder (eds) *Action and Value in Criminal Law*. Oxford: Clarendon.

Turbiner, M. (1961) 'Choice discrimination in schizophrenic and normal subjects for positive, negative and neutral affective stimuli.' *Journal of Consulting Psychology 25*, 92.

Turner, J. (1964) *Russell on Crime, Volume One*. Twelfth edition. London: Stevens.

Turner, J. (1966) *Kenny's Outlines of Criminal Law*. Nineteenth edition. Cambridge: Cambridge University Press.

Uniacke, S. (1994) *Permissible Killing. The Self-Defence Justification of Homicide*. Cambridge: Cambridge University Press.

Van Krevelen, D. (1971) 'Early infantile autism and autistic psychopathy.' *Journal of Autism and Childhood Schizophrenia 1*, 82–86.

Vaughn, C. and Leff, J. (1976) 'The influence of family and social factors on the course of psychiatric illness.' *British Journal of Psychiatry 129*, 125–137.

Walk, A. (1977) 'What we thought about it all.' In D. West and A. Walk (eds) *Daniel McNaughton: His Trial and the Aftermath*. Ashford: Headley.

Walker, N. (1968) *Crime and Insanity in England, Volume One.* Edinburgh: Edinburgh University Press.

Walker, N. (1985) *Sentencing Theory, Law and Practice.* London: Butterworths.

Walker, N. (1991) *Why Punish?* Oxford: Oxford University Press.

Walker, N. (1993) 'McNaughtan's innings: A century and a half not out.' *Journal of Forensic Psychiatry 4,* 207–213.

Walker, N. and McCabe, S. (1973) *Crime and Insanity in England, Volume Two.* Edinburgh: Edinburgh University Press.

Walton, H. and Presly, A. (1973) 'Use of a category system in the diagnosis of abnormal personality.' *British Journal of Psychiatry 122,* 259–268.

Wasik, M. and Pease, K. (1987) 'Discretion and sentencing reform: The alternatives.' In M. Wasik and K. Pease (eds) *Sentencing Reform.* Manchester: Manchester University Press.

Watson, G. (1975) 'Free agency.' *Journal of Philosophy 72,* 205–220.

Waugh, A. (1986) 'Autocastration and biblical delusions in schizophrenia.' *British Journal of Psychiatry 149,* 656–658.

Weihofen, H. (1954) *Mental Disorder as a Criminal Defence.* Buffalo: Dennis.

Weinstock, R. (1976) 'Capgras syndrome: A case involving violence.' *American Journal of Psychiatry 133,* 855.

Wertham, F. (1949) *The Show of Violence.* London: Victor Gollancz.

Wertheimer, M. (1945) *Productive Thinking.* New York: Harper and Bros.

West, D. (1965) *Murder Followed by Suicide.* London: Heinemann.

White, S. (1991) 'Insanity defences and magistrates' courts.' *Criminal Law Review,* 501–509.

Williams, D. (1969) 'Neural factors related to habitual aggression: Consideration of the differences between those habitual aggressive and others who have committed crimes of violence.' *Brain 92,* 503–520.

Williams, G. (1961) *Criminal Law. The General Part.* Second edition. London: Stevens.

Williams, G. (1982) 'The theory of excuses.' *Criminal Law Review,* 732–742.

Williams, G. (1983) *Textbook of Criminal Law.* Second edition. London: Stevens.

Wing, L. (1981) 'Asperger's syndrome: A clinical account.' *Psychological Medicine 11,* 115–129.

Wootton, B. (1959) *Social Science and Social Pathology.* London: George Allen and Unwin.

Wootton, B. (1960) 'Diminished responsibility: A layman's view.' *Law Quarterly Review 76,* 224–239.

Wootton, B. (1963) *Crime and the Criminal Law.* London: Stevens and Sons.

World Health Organisation (WHO) (1978) *Mental Disorders: Glossary and Guide to their Classification in Accordance with the Ninth Revision of the International Classification of Diseases.* Geneva: World Health Organisation.

World Health Organisation (WHO) (1992) *The ICD-10 Classification of Mental and Behavioural Disorders.* Geneva: World Health Organisation.

Wulach, J. (1983) 'Mania and crime: A study of 100 manic defendants.' *Bulletin of the American Academy of Psychiatry and the Law 11,* 69–75.

Yang, C. (1993) 'The insanity defence in China.' *International Bulletin of Law and Mental Health,* July, 8–12.

Yeo, S. (1990) *Compulsion in the Criminal Law.* Sydney: Law Book Company.

Zubin, J. (1975) 'Problem of attention in schizophrenia.' In M. Kietzman, S. Sutton and J. Zubin (eds) *Experimental Approaches to Psychopathology.* New York: Academic Press.

Subject Index

References to endnotes contain the letter "n" preceded by the page number and followed by the endnote number. When cross references are to more than one heading, those headings are separated by semi-colons. When cross references are to sub-headings of other headings, heading and sub-heading are separated by commas.

Author Index